HORSES
and
HELICOPTERS

HORSES
—— *and* ——
HELICOPTERS

*A Son's Tribute to His Father and
Their Shared Military Service*

JIM DOWNEY

HORSES AND HELICOPTERS
A Son's Tribute to His Father and Their Shared Military Service

iUniverse books may be ordered through booksellers or by contacting:

iUniverse LLC
1663 Liberty Drive
Bloomington, IN 47403
www.iuniverse.com
1-800-Authors (1-800-288-4677)

ISBN: 978-1-4917-3431-5 (sc)
ISBN: 978-1-4917-3432-2 (e)

Library of Congress Control Number: 2014908749

Printed in the United States of America.

iUniverse rev. date: 07/09/2014

For my wife, Diann M. Downey, and our fifty-four years of marriage.
In memory of my father and mother.

A father's and son's experiences in World War II and the Republic of Vietnam, as told by the son. Remember—wars are caused by bad politicians, not by soldiers.

Contents

Preface ix
Acknowledgments xi
Introduction xiii

Part 1

1. Horse 101 4
2. Cuckoo Clock.. 5
3. Philippines Trip One... 6
4. Shanghaied to Shanghai 8
5. Return to Field Artillery...11
6. Hitched.. 12
7. First Sergeant Negro Battery 13
8. First Sergeant to Second Lieutenant 15
9. Closest to a Horse, an Indian Motorcycle...................17
10. Sub Pens and One Horse..19
11. Philippines Trip Two..21
12. Letter from My Dad..23
13. Belle Mead General Depot, New Jersey 24
14. Move to Germany 26
15. Honorable Russell B. Long, United States Senate..... 28
16. Return Stateside, Raritan Arsenal, New Jersey............32
17. First Provost Marshal Retired.................................. 34

Part 2

1. Introduction..39
2. Questions 101–122 41
3. Questions 123–143 54
4. Questions 201–233 73
5. Questions 302–328 79
6. Questions 401-422 94
7. Death..104
8. Travel Orders USAF 109
9. Retirement..114

Shortcuts Two

Question   Subject
Number

103   Udorn: Green Footer 41
104   Danang: Free Leave 42
104   Udorn: Wing Hatch..................................43
104   Korat: Welcome Hawaii 44
105   Korat: Hit My Smoke 45
108   Udorn: Shit Hot/TQM..............................47
110   Danang: Rats.. 48
113   Danang: 50 Holier 49
124   Danang: Stag Movie................................ 54
124   Danang: China Beach 56
124   Danang: Bag of Booze 57
125   Danang: Negligee....................................57
127   Danang: Tough on My Kids.................... 58
129   Danang: Army/Anke................................ 59
131   Education Motivation 59
132   Danang: Right Place................................ 60
132   Danang: Conex Box 61
132   Danang: Malaria Pills 60
132 A   Agent Orange 61
133   Awards.. 62
136   Danang: Body Bags 67
138   Danang: Lights Out................................. 70
138   Danang: Finger Muscles.......................... 70
138   Danang: Mule.. 70
138   Udorn: Green Foot Ass 71
138   Korat: Beer Can Mortar 71
305   Udorn: Mig vs. Jolly............................... 79
311   Danang: Naked Fanny/Bent Gear 84
311   Korat: Bull's-Eye 84
402   Udorn: Damn Good 95
402   Udorn: First Chopper/Tail Trouble 95
402   Udorn: APU 95
409   Danang: Crash Crew 98

About the Author 115

Preface

I started this project as a comparison of my father's travels before and during World War II and my travels during the Vietnam conflict. Where did our paths cross? I had received a questionnaire from an air force fighter squadron. While gathering information for the questionnaire, I found my father's military records and photo albums. In his things were also a stack of military orders, papers, and pictures. He had not talked much about his experiences. Thanks to the computer, I was able to enter his orders chronologically, which made it easy to track where he had gone. There was no organization to his documents, so arranging them chronologically worked; the insert function on the computer made it easy. It's too bad my father was not alive to include some personal experiences. He was in the Philippines and China in the 1930s, so our trails crossed on my trips to Vietnam. The questionnaire worked well for me, but it was not always applicable. My father was also in Germany and was one of the few sent back to the Philippines for the planned X-Day invasion of Japan. My travels included Thailand, Laos, and Vietnam—and my travels as an army brat in Europe also simplified following our travels together. Needless to say, I learned a lot about my father's history. I started it in 1994 and worked on it on and off until recently. Why not a book?

Acknowledgments

Thanks to my wife, Diann M. Downey, for her support, love, and caring for the past fifty-four years. And special thanks to our kids and grandkids. Thanks to many teachers throughout my school years in many locations in different countries, states, and levels.

Introduction

Warning: If you expect this document to be about hair, teeth, and eyeballs, you will be disappointed. This is not a shoot, kill, and blow-up-stuff document. It is a running story of two normal people, a father and son who are not in any way heroes. Both gave 110 percent toward every task and endeavor. The real heroes are the ones who gave it their all and returned home in a box—and the ones who came home bent, buckled, and slightly off-center. Those not familiar with military language may have some difficulty understanding some of the abbreviations, especially those from World War II documents. Texters can probably translate the abbreviations with ease.

PART 1

Horses

Major James R. Downey Jr. United States Army (Retired).
From Private to Major

Born: August 26, 1910, in Etna, Tennessee. Died: January 5, 1986.
Blood Type A
Enlisted Member's serial number: 6360147
Officer serial number: 0 498 385 MPC

In 1927, at the age of sixteen years and eleven months, James entered the US Army's Fourth Cavalry to break horses and transition to the field artillery for his first three years of enlistment. His second enlistment, from 1930 to 1933, was as a laboratory technician with Medical Corps, and he was stationed in Manila, Philippines. While there, his duties required him to travel by military ship to Shanghai, China, in early 1932 for an unknown period of time. Photos from his album show numerous pictures with his script notes on some of them. When he went back to the States in 1933, he became the first sergeant of a black artillery battalion at Fort Bragg, North Carolina. Then, in September 1942, he became a second lieutenant in the US Army. On August 17, 1944, he landed at Utah Beach. The following note was in the company history record:

> Lt. Downey, with the First Platoon present at the surrender of the submarine pens at Breast, France, while on a special CIC assignment. This platoon in charge of this installation from date of surrender until relieved by the 156th Infantry.

He then departed Marseille, France, for the Pacific Theater on June 23, 1945, and arrived in Manila, Philippines, on July 28, 1945. This was in preparation for the X-Day invasion of Japan. He returned stateside on November 25, 1945. He then spent three years (July 3, 1948 to January 4, 1952) in Germany with his family as part of the army of occupation. After returning stateside, he was assigned to be the provost marshal of Raritan Arsenal in Metuchen, New Jersey. During that stay he had the opportunity to visit West Point for some unknown purpose. He then retired as a major from the US Army in 1955 to Winter Park, Florida.

Following are excerpts and quotes from military orders. They are in the military's language (military jargon). Of course, there were no computers then, just typewriters. As predecessors to today's texting, they used many abbreviations. Most are obvious. The complicated abbreviations are followed by translations (where known). Many are so old they are no longer listed in military abbreviation lists.

The trooper in the center of the three troopers is James. He is also on the bottom in the picture on the right. Notice the tent in the background of the picture on the right; in part 2, you will see the same model tent thirty-nine years later.

July 29, 1927: Private, LET Hq. Fourth CA. Note: CA is Cavalry. (NPRC) (National Personnel Records Center) (could not find an abbreviation for LET, maybe, Learn Educate Train) July 29, 1927 enlisted through July 28, 1930.

Horse 101: Just from the pictures it is obvious that he is happy and enjoying being a cavalry trooper. He is sixteen, and regardless of anything else, he has met one of his goals. Some of the things a sixteen-year-old would have to learn about horses—how to get on; how to get off; how not to fall off; how not to get on backward; care and feeding of your horse—hoof care, teeth care, mane care, bathing and cleaning, saddle maintenance, etc.; and becoming your horse's best friend. Knowing the army, there was a training manual. It was probably titled *Operations Manual: Horses and Marriage.*

RA, EM 29 July 1927 to 28 July 1930—FA, BTRY Communication (Form 145) (Note: FA is Field Artillery).
October 15, 1929: PFC BO #29 "E" Sixteenth FA (NPRC).

From his handwritten notebook: "While a recruit at Fort Bragg, North Carolina, a carnival stopped in Fayetteville, North Carolina, a nearby town. One of the fellows won a cuckoo clock. He thought it would be fun if he brought it in the barracks just before midnight. At four in the morning the clock started chirping but failed to finish. The next morning, quite a few fellows were late or missed reveille. This was due to having to sort out their boots that were piled up with a busted cuckoo clock in the middle."

He also told this story: "After finishing three months of basic training, several of us were assigned to E. Batry Eighty-Third FA (horse-drawn artillery). One morning at reveille one of the new recruits failed to have his heels of his boots shined. First Sgt. Skippers, a tough soldier, was giving him a rough time when the recruit said in a very low voice, 'Sergeant, you always tell us a good soldier never looks back.'"

Another story I remember he told was about when his army buddies got together. He had demonstrated to locals how well he could shoot when he shot birds with his .45 pistol. What they did not know was that the .45 shells he used contained birdshot. They thought he was a cowboy from the movies.

The following information was obtained from his military record from the National Personnel Records Center in St. Louis, Missouri. The service record was a 4-inch by 8½-inch document, W.D.A.G.O. Form No. 24.

E-16-FA from July 29, 1927 to July 28, 1930. Discharged as Pvt. Character EX. (National Personnel Records Center, (NPRC).

Convicted by Military Court—1929—liquor in barracks—fined $14.00 and reduced in rank.

June 9, 1930: Private S.C.M.O # 54 (NRPC).

August 1, 1930: Reenlisted thru August 5, 1933
RA, EM 29 July 1930 to 4 August 1933—Medical Corps., Laboratory Tech (Form 145).

Med. Dept. from August 1, 1930 to August 5, 1933. Discharged as Pvt. Character VG. Medical Department. Philippines (NPRC).

Foreign Service: Left United States for duty in Manila, Philippines, from Ft. McDowell, California, on November 19, 1930 arrived Manila, Philippines, December 8, 1930, arrived Ft. McDowell, California, on April 7, 1933 (NPRC).

November 27, 1930: Thanksgiving dinner aboard the US Army Transport *US Grant*, built in 1907 in Stettin, Germany, for the Hamburg American line and designed for tropical service in the run between Hamburg and Buenos Aires. It was known as the *Koenig Wilhelm 11* while under the German flag. At the opening of the World War, the ship was interned at Hoboken and later confiscated as alien property on our entrance into the conflict. After being renamed *The Madawaska*, the ship was in the Transport Service for over eighteen months and earned the right to wear the three gold chevrons, which still adorn the funnel to this day. When troop movements incidental to the cessation of hostilities had been completed, the vessel was turned back to the control of the United States Shipping Board and a year later was again assigned to the War Department for permanent use as a transport, and renamed the *US Grant*. Two years ago the interior of the ship was completely refitted with the view of increasing the passenger-carrying capacity, and it is now the flagship of the transport fleet. The general dimensions of the ship are as follows: length overall, 508 feet; depth, 34 feet; gross tonnage, 9,410; net tonnage, 5,640; displacement, 15,010 tons. It is equipped with the gyroscope compass, automatic steering device, mechanical depth finder, submarine signal apparatus, hydroelectric steering gear, and the latest types of marine generators and electric lifeboat davits. There are 240 officers and men in the crew.

February 7, 1932: The entire three and a half miles of front lines had been barbwired and sandbagged with machine guns ready. The battle for Chapei lasted until March 3, and neither the Chinese nor the Japanese encroached on the International Settlement, but from their front lines, the Fourth Marines had grandstand seats for the war (from http://www.chinamarines.com/docs/shan.htm).

Note: Pictures found in my father's photo albums indicated that he was in China somewhere around this point in time—for what purpose I haven't found out yet. Guess: as he was a laboratory technician, is it possible he was sent VOCO (Verbal Order of Commander) TDY (Temporary Duty) to Shanghai, China, in support of the Fourth Marine's hospital?

I wrote a letter to Mr. Frank J. Kossyta, 3710 Arthiem St., San Diego, California 92111. His letter dated June 6, 2004 (D-Day) contained the following: "Dear James, pictures were taken. (Had sent him copies of pictures showing marines in Shanghai.) In early part of the year of 1932, city of Shanghai was International Settlement of four foreign countries. They were Great Britain, France, Italy, and Japan in 1932. Shanghai was the object, the Japanese Landing Forces. The Japanese landed at Kiwang and Woosung areas. Located about ten miles Southeast of Shanghai, China the International Settlement of Shanghai was governed by these countries. In their concession, assisted by a military force. Local police forces and body politic. China had special areas in the city of Shanghai. The United States Marine Corps leased their areas from China. The USMC Fourth Marines Infantry Regiment was stationed in the city of Shanghai. The US Army, Thirty-First Infantry Regiment was stationed in the city of Manila, on the Island of Luzon, Philippines Islands. The army location was in the area called Wall City. The army sent troops to Shanghai, China in 1932 to reinforce USMC Fourth Marines. Later I spoke to a few army soldiers that made the expedition to China. I marked pictures #1 and #2 US Army personnel identified by wrap leggings, and lengthwise overcoats. Marines wore canvas leggings and knee-length overcoats. Campaign hat with regimental insignia badge. Thirty-First Infantry insignia badge was a white dragon on purple enamel background. The US Military transported forward supplies, military personnel on itinerary. Returned to United States Army to San Francisco, docked at Fort Mason, transferred to Fort McDowell, which was on Angel Island in San Francisco Bay." *Signature.* P.S. And written note at the end indicated, "I am ninety-one years old. I spent time in Fort McKintey—Philippines Scout Training Camp and about sixty years in China with the US Army & Marines Corp."

Chinese troops Chapei, Kiangwan, Shanghai.

February 5, 1932: *Montreal Daily Star.* E-mail from despower @ shawcable.com, who has been very helpful in providing information. I also sent him some of the pictures. Part of the article follows:

Seven United States destroyers arrived from Manila. The transport Chaumont with a thousand troops was due before nightfall. The British and American warships anchored in the Whangpoo River in the heart of the city, greeted by the deafening roars of heavy gunfire, which rocked the city in the renewed Japanese onslaught. *Powers Concentrate*: their arrival was part of the concentration in the war zone by these two major powers. They led the way for others, chiefly French and Italian, also mobilizing here, to protect lives of their endangered nations. The Chinese troops suffered tremendous losses, Japanese reports indicated that ten Japanese airplanes loaded with high explosives bombs flew low over Chapet. They opened up with machine guns over dwindling lines of Chinese, fighting desperately amid ruins of blackened buildings. The Japanese advance was on two fronts. They moved into a Japanese cemetery with their right wing in the Chapet drive. The left concentrated on the North Station area. The Chinese were between the Japanese pincers. Their ammunition appeared low. None was being brought up. The aircraft carrier Hosho dispatched additional airplanes to cooperate with the attacking air fleet. Admiral Koichi Shlosawa, still in command, appeared determined to—. (The second part was not legible.)

Quotes from *China's Trial by Fire: The Shanghai War of 1932*, by Donald A. Jordan, The University of Michigan Press.

Page 30: "A destroyer from the US Naval Base at Manila had arrived only days earlier to join the one already on station. On January 28, four additional destroyers carrying 425 troops steamed out bound for Shanghai to strengthen the two thousand US Marines that contributed settlement defense system."

USS Houston

Page 63: "The response of the State Department was to take issue with Tokyo's military operations, which endangered the entire port of Shanghai, where some four thousand Americans resided and where the United States had great interest."

Page 48: "In the initial Japanese attack from transiting through the S.V.C. checkpoint on Honan Road to flank the North Station. Later on, January 29, became necessary for the S.V.C. to make a show of force to keep a band of Chinese soldiers from entering the settlement in the western district. British employees of the Shanghai Nanking Railroad found themselves stranded on trains outside the settlement as Japanese flyers bombed the tracks west of Chapei in an attempt to interdict reinforcement."

Page 71: "Not satisfied with just petitioning for war, by January 30 the GLU was organizing workers, presumably the unemployed or strikers, to help the Red Cross carry the wounded back to Shanghai hospitals and military medical centers."

Page 72: "The SLPPA participants claimed to have solicited ten thousand quilts and ten thousand padded coats for the troops and the many displaced refugees that had to endure the late winter chill."

Page 89: "On February 3, Admiral Shiozawa issued warnings to the *USS Houston* and *HMS Sandwich* to steer clear of the barrage. Much to the delight of the Chinese leadership, the Western powers called in more warships, anchoring them along the Settlement Bund on standby to protect their own nationals."

Page 94: "Newly arriving US and British warships placed themselves in the Yangtze between the Japanese and Chinese naval vessels, which had agreed to a tenuous nonengagement. Britain's China Squadron now included Admiral Kelley's *HMS Kent*, five cruisers, and numerous destroyers and gunboats. The US Asiatic Fleet commander, Admiral Taylor, aboard his flagship, the cruiser *USS Houston*, had steamed in from the Philippines amid a convoy of destroyers plus a transport laden with fourteen hundred infantrymen and marines. The Western military presence at the Shanghai conflict received front page coverage in the world press."

Page 231: "With the controversies answered, a deputation of the British consulate went to the several hospitals in the international settlement where the battered negotiators could affix their signatures."

Obviously not dressed for weather in the Philippines.

October 24, 1933: Reenlisted through October 23, 1936
RA, EM 24 October 1933 to 23 October 1937—FA, Fire control instrument and supplies.

1933: AWOL One to five days confinement.

E-83-FA from October 24, 1933 to October 23, 1936, discharged as Corp. Character EX (NPRC).

September 26, 1934: W.D., A/G.O. Form No. 58. Private First Class James R. Downey Jr., 6360147 hereby appointed Corporal, Battery E, Eighty-Third FA.

Completed C.W.S., (Chemical Warfare) Fourth C.A. Rating: 81 percent. 1935 (NPRC).

November 28, 1935: Thanksgiving dinner, Battery "E" Eighty-Third Field Artillery, Fort Bragg, North Carolina. Menu: Oyster Soup Oysteretes Celery Hearts Sweet Mixed Pickles Ripe Olives Shrimp Salad Sliced Tomatoes Roast Turkey Oyster Dressing Virginia Ham Cranberry Sauce Giblet Gravy Whipped Irish Potatoes Buttered June Peas Candied Yams Creamed Corn Parker House Rolls Butter Ice Cream Mince Pie Coconut Pumpkin Pie Fruit Cake Coconut Layer Cake Oranges Apples Bananas Grapes Mixed Nuts Assorted Candies Coffee Fruit Punch Apple Cider Milk Sugar Cigars Cigarettes. Mess Sergeant: D.H. Upchurch. Mess Officer: 2nd Lt. Hugh M. Exton. Roster included as Corporals, James R. Downey.

February 28, 1936: Certificate of Proficiency. This is to certify that Corporal James R. Downey Jr., Battery "E" Eighty-Third FA, Ft. Bragg, North Carolina has successfully completed the fourth Corps Area Special Correspondence Course in Chemical Warfare for unit gas personnel with a rating of 81.

October 25, 1936: Reenlisted through November 10, 1942.
Ra, EM 24 October 1937 to 11 November 1942—FA, Motor Sgt. & First Sgt. AUS 11 November, 1942 to date. Personnel adjutant, Company Off. and Company Commander. Schools—Field Artillery, chemical warfare, Corps of Military Police Forces.

October 25, 1936-20 BN. Eighty-Third FA. E Battery (NPRC)
Eighty-Third FA from October 25, 1939 to October 24, 1939, discharged as Corp. Character EX. Under the minimum wt. by three (3) lbs. Waiver approved per ltr. Hq. Ft. Bragg, North Carolina dated October 21, 1939 (NPRC).

March 9, 1937: Headquarters, Second Battalion, Eighty-Third Field Artillery Commendation of enlisted men on flood relief duty. The Battalion Commander desires to express his appreciation for the fine manner in which the following men of the battalion conducted themselves while on flood relief duty. Cpl. James R. Downey, E Battery. Most favorable reports have been received from all concerned and the high order of performance of duty under the unusual conditions, which was observed, and has brought great credit to the battalion.

March 11, 1937: married to Thisbe W. Chandler of Mckenzie Tennessee (age twenty-four), his age twenty-six. State of South Carolina Dillon County Probate Court. Matrimony by B. Frank Edwards, H.P. for South Carolina.

March 30, 1937: Battery E Eighty-Third Field Artillery, Fort Bragg, North Carolina. Subject: Credit of enlisted man. 1. Request the following named man of this organization be allowed monthly credit at the Quartermaster Sales Store and activities to the amount set opposite his name: Corporal James R. Downey Jr.—Subsistence $15.00 Total $15.00. 2. Corporal Downey is married and lives off the Post. 3. The above soldier has never had commissary credit before. 4. Rate of pay per month: $46.20.

W.D., A.G.O. Form No. 58. Corporal James R. Downey Jr., 6360147 hereby appointed *Sergeant, Btry C, Eighty-Third, G.A.

December 25, 1937: Christmas Battery "E" Eighty-Third Field Artillery Fort Bragg, North Carolina. Menu: Sweet Mixed Pickles Sliced Tomatoes Stuffed Olives Roast Pork Roast Turkey Cranberry Sauce Candied Sweet Potatoes Giblet Gravy Sage Dressing Headed Lettuce Celery Hearts Buttered June Peas Fruit Cake Apples Mince Meat Pies Oranges Assorted Nuts Grapes Peanuts Beer Pretzels Coffee Milk Sugar Parker House Rolls Butter Cigars Cigarettes Mess Officer: 2nd Lt. Philip G. Lauman Jr. Mess Sergeant: Duby H. Upchurch. Roster: Cpl. James R. Downey Jr.

March 8, 1939: born one son, Fort Bragg, North Carolina. James R. Downey III.

November 21, 1940: Battery "E" Eighty-Third Field Artillery, Fort Jackson, South Carolina. Thanksgiving Dinner: Celery Mixed Pickles Lettuce and Tomato Salad Roast Young Turkey Cranberry Sauce Giblet Gravy Oyster Dressing Virginia Baked Ham Creamed Peas Candied

Yams Steamed Rice Parker House Rolls Butter Mince Meat Pie Chocolate Layer Cake Coconut Layer Cake Fruit Punch Coffee Oranges Apples Grapes Assorted Candies Nuts Cigars Cigarettes. Mess Officer: 2nd Lt. S.B. Teague. Mess Sergeant: Duby H. Upchurch. Roster included Supply Sergeant James R. Downey Jr.

December 25, 1940: Battery "E" Eighty-Third Field Artillery, Fort Jackson, South Carolina. Menu: Celery Mixed Pickles Lettuce and Tomato Salad Roast Young Turkey Cranberry Sauce Giblet Gravy Oyster Dressing Virginia Baked Ham Creamed Peas Candied Yam Steamed Rice Parker House Rolls Butter Mince Meat Pie Chocolate Layer Cake Oranges Apples Grapes Coconut Layer Cake Fruit Punch Coffee Assorted Candies Nuts Cigars Cigarettes Mess Officer: 2nd Lt. J.V. Sherlock Mess Sergeant: Duby H. Upchurch. Roster lists sergeants including James R. Downey Jr.

March 1, 1941: Headquarters Fifth FA Training Regiment, Fort Bragg, North Carolina. Under the provisions of AR 615-5 and upon recommendation of the battalion and battery commander, the following appointment and promotion of non-commissioned officers in Battery E, Sixteenth Battalion, are announced. To be Staff Sergeant: Sgt. James R. Downey Jr., #630147, Vice St. Sgt. Mayo promotion.

March 1, 1941: W.D., A.G.O. Form No. 58. Sergeant James R. Downey Jr., 6360147 hereby appointed *Staff Sergeant, Btry E, Sixteenth Bn, Fifth FA Tng Regiment.

June 28, 1941: Certificate Good Conduct Medal. This is to certify that James R. Downey Jr., First Sgt, 6360147 Battery A Fifteenth Battalion, Fifth Field Artillery Training Regiment, Field Artillery Replacement Training Center, Fort Bragg, North Carolina, who completed three years continuous active Federal Service with character excellent June 28, 1941, is entitled to wear the Good Conduct Medal authorized by Army Regulation 600-68, dated October 18, 1941, as modified by circular No. 104, War Department, dated April 9, 1941.

July 26, 1941: Finance Office US Army. First check in payment of this allotment will be mailed September 2, 1941, Jefferson Standard Life Ins. Co., Greensboro, North Carolina. $9.38 for fourteen months.

November 21, 1941: W.D., A.G.O. Form No. 58; Staff Sergeant (temporary) Btry E, Sixteenth Bn., 5th FATR Hereby appointed *First Sergeant (temporary) Btry E, Sixteenth Bn., Fifth FATR

Note: Battery E, Sixteenth Bn, Fifth FATR, Field Training Regiment) was a Negro (colored) battery as was the entire Sixteenth Bn. Cadre for Battery E, Sixteenth Battalion came from the Seventieth Field Artillery Battalion, Fort Jackson, South Carolina. Reference: *Historical and Pictorial Review*, Fifth Regiment Field Artillery Replacement Training Center, Fort Bragg, North Carolina, 1941, The Army and Navy Publishing Company, Inc.

December 7, 1941: Pearl Harbor

February 2, 1942: Headquarter 791st Military Police Battalion (ZI) Camp Gordon, Georgia, 2. I was paid at Fort Oglethorpe, Georgia for the period from November 12, 1942 to November 30, 1942, inclusive, while attending the PMGTS.

February 29, 1942: HQ. Fifth FA TNG Regt FT Bragg, North Carolina, July 23, 1942. To: C. G. F.A. Repl TNG. Center 1. Approved.

2. Statement of Service: Sixteenth FA from July 29, 1927 to July 28, 1930 discharged as Pvt Character EX by reason of ETS. Med Dept. from August 1, 1930 to August 5, 1933 discharged as Pvt Character VG by reason of ETS. Eighty-Third FA from October 24, 1933 to October 23, 1936 discharged as Corp. Character EX by reason of ETS. Eighty-Third FA from October 25, 1936 to October 24, 1939 discharged as Corp Character EX By reason of ETS. Enlisted at Fort Bragg, North Carolina October 25, 1939 in grade of Corporal. Appointed First Sergeant November 21, 1941.

September 1, 1942: W.D., A.G.O. Form No. 58; First Sergeant James R. Downey Jr. #6360147 hereby appointed Master Sergeant (Temporary) Btry. A Fifteenth Bn., Fifth FATR.

September 29, 1942: War Department The Adjutant General's Office Washington

AG 201 Downey, James Richard Jr. (September 29, 1942) BM Subject: Temporary Appoint, Through: Commanding Officer, Fort Bragg, North Carolina. A 0-498385 First Sgt. James Richard Downey Jr., U.S.A.

Btry A, Fifteenth Bn., Fifth FA Tng. Regy. Fort Bragg, North Carolina. (Temp. Appointed 2nd Lt. AUS) 1. By direction of the president you are temporarily appointed and commissioned in the Army of the United States, effective this date, in the grade and section shown in address above. Your serial number is shown after A above. 2. This commission will continue in force during the pleasure of the President of the United States for the time being and for the duration of the present emergency and six months thereafter unless sooner terminated. 3. There is enclosed herewith a form for oath of office, which you are requested to execute and return promptly to the agency from which it was received. The execution and return of the required oath of office constitute an acceptance of your appointment. No other evidence of acceptance is required. 4. This letter should be retained by you as evidence of your appointment, as no commissions will be issued during the war. 5. Separate instruction as to your discharge and issuance of active duty orders will be issued. By order of the Secretary of War: /S/ J A ULIO Major General The Adjutant General.

First Sgt. James R. Downey Jr. Battery AA, Fifteenth FA. Training Center Fort Bragg, North Carolina. Dear Sergeant Downey: Upon acceptance of the commission herewith tendered, you will make your arrangements so as to arrive at Fort Oglethorpe, Georgia, on November 14, 1942, for temporary duty as a student in the Provost Marshal General's Refresher School, Tenth Class. This slip will be handed to the receiving officer upon your arrival at Fort Oglethorpe.

September 30, 1942: War Department, Washington, excerpt. dp Following officer ordered to ad wp from home station on date indicated. tdn. fd 31 p 431-01, 02 03 07 08, a 0425-23. All dates are 1942 and personnel of AUS unless otherwise indicated: 2nd Lt. James Richard Downey Jr. 0498385, Dickson, Tenn. (Now at Ft. Bragg, North Carolina) Eff. Date of Duty: 11 November Branch and Station to which Assigned CMP, PMG Sch Gen, Ft Oglethorpe. Ga (TPA) Date of Rank 11 November.

November 3, 1942: Hq. Fifth FA Training Regiment, Fort Bragg, North Carolina First Sgt. Downey D-14.

January 22, 1943. The Provost Marshal General's School Fort Custer Michigan Corps of Military Police. This is to certify that Second Lieutenant James R. Downey Jr. 0498385 has successfully completed the course of instruction in the Refresher Course.

February 9, 1943: Office of the Finance Officer, Fort Custer, Michigan, James R. Downey Jr., 2nd Lt., 791st MP Bn. (ZI), Camp Gordon, Georgia. The record of this office indicates that this office paid Lt. James R. Downey Jr. for the month of December 1942 as follows: Base and longevity pay (Vou .#4833*) $150.00. Substance allowance: $43.40. Rental allowance: $60.00. Total credit: $253.40. Deduct for class E allotment $9.38. Net Paid: $244.02.

May 11, 1943: War Department Washington excerpt Par. 15 Announcement is made of the temp promotion of the following named officers to the grade indicated in the AUS with fr date of this order. 2nd Lt. to 1st Lt. James Richard Downey Jr. 0498385 AUS.

March 20, 1943: Hq. Camp Gordon, Georgia, Previously recommended for promotion: 12. State how, when, and where the officer has demonstrated his fitness for promotion. State full reasons why any exception to announced policy (if requested or indicated) is warranted in his case. (Par. 9b (3), Sect. I, Cir. 161, W. D., 1942. Second Lieutenant Downey has clearly demonstrated his fitness for the responsibilities and duties of the position and grade of First Lieutenant in an excellent manner. He has displayed outstanding qualities of leadership and proven himself to be well qualified, very capable, efficient, and outstanding in the performance of his duties. He reported to this organization February 1, 1943 and organized the personnel section in an excellent manner. Since that time he has done an outstanding job as Personnel Adjutant of this battalion. He has over sixteen years' service as an enlisted man in the regular army, most of which time he was Motor Sergeant, Signal Sergeant, Supply Sergeant, First Sergeant, and Sergeant Major. He graduated from the Provost Marshal General's School January 22, 1943. In comparison with other officers, I consider him in the upper (1/3) one-third.

October 19, 1943: Headquarters 725th Military Police Battalion (ZI) 2. First lieutenant James R. Downey Jr., 0-498385, will proceed from this station to Beaufort, South Carolina, with two trucks with four drivers and cargo for prisoner of War Camp at that point. Upon completion of this duty they will return to home station.

November 10, 1943: Army Service Forces Fourth Service Command 725th Military Police Battalion (ZI). Under the provisions of paragraph 6a, (1), AR 605-115, as changed by circular #18, War Department, dated 22 January 1942, First Lieutenant James R. Downey Jr., 0498385 is granted leave of absence for ten (10) days, effective on or about 11 November 1943.

December 25, 1943: 1st Lt., HQ 725th M.P. Bn (ZI), Fort McPherson, Georgia.

Merry Christmas, Battalion Mess 791st Military Police Battalion. Menu: Cream Celery Soup aux Croutons Roast Vermont Turkey Sage Dressing Giblet Sauce Snowflake Potatoes Baked Squash Creamed Corn Lettuce Salad Russian Dressing Hot Rolls Bread Butter Mince Pie Chocolate Cake Assorted Fruits Coffee Candy Nuts Cigarettes.

December 27, 1943: Confidential: Army Service Forces Fourth Service Command, Fort Jackson, South Carolina 22. All personnel and equipment of the 725th MP Bn (ZI) (less Co B), this sta, are trfd in gr to sta Comp, 1458th SCU, this sta, effective this date. EM are atchd unasgd to MP Sub=Sect, Sect #1, HQ Det, Sta Comp; Officers are asgd to Hq, Sta Comp. (Auth: Confidential Ltr [AG 322 = Military Police], Hq Fourth SvC, 23 December 1943.)

Both pictures taken in England. They are Indian
(not Harley Davidson) motorcycles.

January 20, 1944: Restricted Army Service Forces, Headquarters, Fourth Service Command, Atlanta 3, Georgia Special Orders No. 17 30.

Following O reld asgmt and dy sta indicated asgd sta indicated, WP: 1st Lt. James R. Downey Jr. 0498385 CMP, RELD FR, Atchd unasgt Sta Com FT Jackson, SC. Asgd to: 795th MP Bn (ZI) Ft. Jackson, South Carolina. Envelope: War Department HQ. 791st. m.p. Bn. (ZI) Fort McPherson, Georgia, Official Business. To, 1st Lt. James R. Downey Jr., HQ. 725th M.P. Bn. (ZI) Fort Jackson, South Carolina.

Company B 795th Military Police Battalion, Pacific Theater of Operations APO 75, US Army Roster of Officers & Enlisted men of this Company with home address. (List contains about 120 names.) First on the list James R. Downey Jr., 1st Lt., 0-498385, 104 High Street Dickson, Tennessee.

February 14, 1944: University of Florida—General Extension Division Certificate of Achievement: This is to certify that James R. Downey Jr. has complied with attendance and achievement requirements of Basic Procedure in Law Enforcement, a training course offered by the General Extension Division of the University of Florida.

June 6, 1944: D-Day

August 26, 1944: Headquarters VIII Corps CIC Detachment #208 Landerneau, 1st Lt. James R. Downey and thirty-four men are reporting for Temporary Duty to be used only for CIC during the present operation. Upon completion of duty, 1st Lt. James R. Downey will return to his proper station. Note: Only Landerneau found in search is in France.

September 28, 1944: Company B 795th Military Police Battalion. Subject History, 1944. 30 May 1944. The company boarded transport ship BO-711 en route for overseas destination. 3 June sailed from Boston Harbor. 11 June 1944 arrived Greenock, Scotland. 12 June 1944 arrived Tidworth, Wilts, England. To Parkhouse, Camp B., 16 June 1944: arrived Totnes, South Devon, England to Camp W-2. 20 June 1944 arrived Torquay. The company relieved the 707th Military Police Battalion, and assumed Military Police duties in Torquay. This assignment considered temporary. Detachments were formed and proceeded to the following towns. To relieve the 707th Military Police Battalion, Brixham, Totness, Dartmouth, Kingsbridge, Buchfastleigh, Ashburton, and Newton Abbot. Duties included control of troops in the towns, assignment of auxiliary Military Police, and Providing Convoy Escort. 16 August 1944, the company boarded the *Empire Lance*, en route to France. 17 August 1944, the company landed at UTAH Beach, and marched to Bivouac area. 19 August 1944, the company departed from the UTAH Beach bivouac areas and arrived at Mont St. Michel. 25 August 1944 Mission with Eighth Corps assigned to B Company. Lt. Downey, with First Platoon departed for St. Renan. 28 September 1944 the First Platoon returned from St. Renan. Activities: Lt. Downey, with First Platoon present at the surrender of the submarine Pens at Brest. The platoon in charge of this installation from date of surrender until relieved by 156th Infantry.

"A pin-up boy" and yours truly,   *Jan. '45 France*
France 9 Nov. '44

Hitler's U-boat bases, Jak P. Mallmann Showell, Naval Institute Press, Annapolis, Maryland Copyright @ 2002 Jak P. Mallmann Showell.

Page 33 next to a picture: "In and around Brest there were at least fifty-two 103mm or larger and sixteen 88mm anti-aircraft guns, as well as a multitude of smaller caliber weapons to cope with low level attacks."

Page 52 next to picture: "The Brest bunker seen from the sea. Although the biggest building in the area, the huge concrete monstrosity is dwarfed by the hill behind with the naval school on the top. This entire area consists of hard rock, which has been hollowed out with tunnels leading to underground workshops, storerooms, and fuel reservoirs."

Page 93 mid page: "The German garrison in Brest, together with several workers from the Todt Organization, surrendered to American troops on 21 September 1944, and shortly afterward the French navy moved in to supervise the clearing up of the devastation in the dock yard."

Note conflict with above departure date.

March 20, 1945: Headquarters 795th Military Police Battalion European Theater of Operations APO 339, US Army. Subject Award of Meritorious Service Unit Plaque. All Members 795th Military Police Battalion, APO 339, US Army.

May 8, 1945: V-E Day (Victory in Europe)

(31) Arr Etousa 11 June 1944 EAME ribbon Per Par 3 SO 76 Hq 795 MP Bn 10 July 1944. Dep Southhampton, Eng 17 August 1944. Arr Utah Bch France 17 August 1944. Qual to wear one overseas Bar 2 December 1944. Departed France 14 March 1945.Arrived Holland 14 March 1945. Departed Holland 18 March 1945. Arrived Germany 18 March 1945. Participation Cmpn Northern France GO3. Hq 795 MP Bn 5 April 1945. Physical Profile (1) 213111x (Class C) 18 May 1945, Co B, 795 Mp Bn. 94-yes-42.2 (JRD) (Ref 15-Comm AUS 11 November 1942) Dep Germany 26 May 1945. Arr France 27 May 1945. Dep Marseille, Fr. For Pacific Theater 23 June 1945, Arr Manila, P.I. 28 July 1945. Atzd Bz Serv Star (Central Europe (Ltr 5. Hq *Etousa* Ag 2000.6 OPGA, 27 June 1945. Atzd Bz Serv Star (Rhineland), @d Ind, Hq *Etousa* 23 June 1945. To Ltr, Hq 9 Army, File 200.6 (BPG) GNMAG, 13 June 1945. Atzd Asiatic—Pacific Theater Ribbon. WD Cir 62, 1944, Atzd American Defense Ribbon, WD Cir 27, 1944. Atzd Philippine Liberation Ribbon WD Cir 136, 1945 (NPRC). Letter from National Personnel Records Center. January 31, 2008.

> *American Defense Service Medal*;
> *American Campaign Medal*;
> *Asiatic-Pacific Campaign Medal*;
> *European-African-Middle Eastern Campaign Medal* with three bronze service stars;
> *World War II Victory Medal*;

Army of Occupation Medal with Germany clasp;
National Defense Service Medal;
Philippine Liberation Ribbon;
Sharpshooter Badge with pistol bar

August 6, 1945: V-J Day (Victory in Japan)

August 14, 1945: Manila, Philippines. Letter from Dad. Dear Son: Well it looks as though it won't be long now before we can go hunting and fishing. I have already asked your mother if she wanted to be our dog. Ha. You can tell mother to break out now with the dough that we are going to get that electric train and beaucoup (a bunch) tracks, maybe to engines. What? Don't have much time to write now—just wanted to drop you a line to let you know won't be long now. Love. Your Dad. Return address: Lt. Jas R. Downey Jr. 0498385 Co "B" 795th M.P. Bn. A.P.O. 75% Philippines. San. (Note: 75 percent of all letters were opened and passed by examiners. "Loose Lips Sink Ships.")

August 21, 1945: Headquarters 795th Military Police Battalion Pacific Theater of Operations, APO 75, US Army Certificate. I certify that the following officers are authorized to wear a Bronze Service Star on the European—African—Middle Eastern—Theater Ribbon for campaigns indicate (*) opposite their name; 1st Lt. James R. Downey Jr. 0 498 385 Northern France (*) Rhineland (*) Central Europe (*).

September 30, 1945: I certify that I left the United States 3 June 1944 (Pay Voucher) Thisbe C. Downey, PO Box 166, McKenzie, Tennessee. Note on back of photo: Manila P.I. 15 September 1945.

In 1930 he was stationed at Manila. It is 1945 and "he's back."

October 8, 1945: Restricted Headquarter Military Police Command AFWESPAC; Fol named Off, orgns as indicated, are reld asgmt and dy and atchd unsagd to Repl Depot, APO 238, for the purpose of receiving further orders for return to the United States in connection with release from active dy or reasgmt in accordance with WD Readjustment Regulations. EDCMR 10 October 1945. TC will furnish necessary T. WP. TDN. (Tvl by govt mtr T Twenty-Ninth Repl Depot is auth) Auth: Rad CG AFWESPAC GX 11171 GSXRS, dtd 13 Sep 45). (Race—All White) Name First Lt. James R. Downey Jr. ASN 0498385 AorS CMP ASPS 102 Organization 795th MP BN APO 75.

October 10, 1945: Medical Detachment 795th Military Police Battalion APO 75 c/o Postmaster, San Francisco, California. Certificate: I hereby certify that 1st Lt. James R. Downey WNEY 0-4983385 has completed all immunization required by Par 2 i. (1) (2) Circular No.32, General Headquarters, United States Army Forces, Pacific, APO 500, dated 2 August 1945.

October 23, 1945: CO AFWESPAC SGC STYER: The following radio received from War Department is quoted for your information pending publication of War Department Circular announcement. Here By Made American, Theater Ribbon may be awarded to all United States Military personnel who serves honorably on active duty in continental United States for accumulated period of one year including permanent and temporary duty during World War II commencing 7 December 1941.

October 25, 1945: headquarter 795th military Police Battalion, Pacific Theater of Operations APO 75, US Army Personnel of this Bn entitled to wear the Philippine Liberation Ribbon are authorized to wear one (1) bronze service star on the ribbon, Auth Par 2 b (2) Cir 91, AFPAC. Dtd 12 October 1945.

November 25, 1945: Army Service Forces, San Francisco Port of Embarkation Camp Stoneman, Pittsburgh, California 35. Fol RS and Sep C Gps at str indicated WP WDPC o/a 27 November 45 by rail (Main 45159); The movement constitutes a permanent change of sta for ea individual. The QMCwill provide necessary ki car (transportation) facilities and rat for off and EM for number of days indicated as provided in WD Cir 400, 44. The Transportation off Cp (Camp) Stoneman will furnish shipping containers and govt B/L. Ki car equip will be returned to CP Stoneman UP Par, AR 55-135 Transportation Off UP AR 30-2215 will provide meal tickets as

indicated for EM Shown. Upon compl (completion) of TDY (temporary duty) OFF (officers) and EM (enlisted men) placed on TDY as Tn Comdr and Mess Rscort Person will ret this sta. Ret tvl by commercial aircraft for TN Comdr is auth if practicable. TTC, TCT. TDN. 601-31 P 433-02 A 212-60425 S99-999 fr (from) Cp Stoneman Downey, James R Jr. 0-498385 1st Lt. CC 684 RN 110 SSN 9110
ASR102 104 High St. Dickson Tennessee. (Orders sent to that address.)

December 6, 1945: Headquarters Reception Station 15 Fort McPherson, Georgia. Fol Off having ret US and rptd this Hq in compliance auth appearing below name are reld fr overseas asgmt and fr atchd unsgd this sta and adgd in gr to org and sta indicated for duty. Off granted forty-five days TDY for rest and recuperation. Upon completion of TDY Off will rpt new sta on or before date indicated. Tyl time indicated granted. UP AR 35-4820 dtd 19 April 1945 per diem will be paid for period of tyl. No per diem will be paid for period of recuperation. TCT PCS TDN TPA FSA. 601-31 P 431-02-03 A 212/60425 S99-999 AUTH: WD Memo 600-45 and WD Ltr file AG 370.5 16 August 1944 PRI as amended. Ltr Subj 210.31/5624 (15 July 1945) GNGAP-P Hq AGF Wash 25 DC 5 September 1945. This order constitutes a PCS with TDY en route home for recuperation. EDCMR 11 December 1945. Downey, James R. Jr. 0498385. 1st Lt. CMP 5 25 January, 104 High St. Dickson Tenn. (2d Ind Pers Center Receiving Div Ft McPherson Ga 6 December 1945). Note: above orders were for rest and recuperation between the war in Europe and travel to the Philippines to prepare for the invasion of Japan.

December 10, 1945: France, letter to me: "My Dearest Little Man + Son. Received your nice letter today telling me what all Santa brought. My goodness, he must have left his bag there with you, all those things you got. How are you and the skates doing now? Who is winning—your fanny or the skates? Ha, you be careful and don't break any bones. Mother sent me your tooth. I'm going to keep it on my dog tag chain. She said you put it under your pillow and found a nickel the next morning. Well, you be a good little man and watch out for mother all so you love her for me until love her. Yours, Dad. Here is some money for you—German & French— bet mother don't have any like it. Dad." Note: date has to be 1944.

Return address: Lt Jas R. Downey Jr. 0498385 Co "B" 795th M.P. Bn APO 517 % Postmaster NYC, New York.

January 6, 1946: Headquarters Station 15: 25. So much of par 15 of special Orders 340 this HQ dtd 1945 pertaining to 1st Lt. James R. Downey Jr. as reads Asgd ORP Ft. Sam Houston, Texas is amended to read: sgd SvC PW Base Camp Belle Mead ASF Depot Belle Mead, New Jersey. Authority: twx tac spxpo—A-C 6 January 1946.

February 25, 1946: Army Service Forces Belle Mead Army Service Forces Depot; 1. 1st Lt. James R. Downey Jr., in add to his other duties, detailed as C! B Agent) to Col C. K. McAllister, FD, FOUSA, New York, New York, Vice CWO Benjamin A. Heriot, W2109195, USA, reld, eff this date. (Auth: Par 3b, AR 35-320.)

March 21, 1946: ASF Fourth Service Command Records Depot, Atlanta 3, Georgia: Orders transferring you from the 725th MP Bn to 795th MP Bn, Fort Jackson, South Carolina could not be found, but a statement to the effect that your name did appear on the 795th MP Bn's final roster upon departure from this station for Ft. Custer, Michigan, is submitted in lieu thereof.

April 9, 1946: Army Service Forces Headquarters Second Service Command, Governor's Island NY 4 New York. Fol-named offd are detailed as Actg Asst Insp Gen at stas indicated for purpose of receiving complaints in accordance w/prov of Sec II WD Cir 74 14 March 1946 off 9 April 1946 in addition to their other duties: 1st Lt. James R. Downey Jr. CMP BMASFD Belle Mead, New Jersey.

May 2, 1946: To Army and Navy Journal, Inc. 1711 Connecticut Avenue Northwest. Dear Sirs: Change #1, Par. 5b, AR 35-2420, dated 12 April 1946 is rather vague to several of the regular army enlisted men. Would appreciate it very much if you would clarify it more. My present status is as follows: In 1930 I reenlisted and received seventy-five dollars as enlisted allowance. In 1933 and 1936 I reenlisted without the allowance. In 1939 I reenlisted and received $150 enlistment allowance. Was due for discharge in 1942 but was held in service and given a commission, which I have held since that time. No time lost under A.W. 107. No breaks in service over thirty days. Have completed eighteen years as of 24 October 1945. If my commission was terminated 24 October 1946, how much enlistment allowance would I be entitled to for the above stated service?

June 4, 1946: Belle Mead General Depot, United States Army, Belle Mead, New Jersey, 2. Ord lv of absence for ten (10) days plus five (5) days travel time, eff O/a 24 June 1946, granted 1st Lt. James R. Downey Jr., 0498385, CMP. Par 23b, AR 605-115 requires ea off to keep a personal record of lv used. Par 27b, AR 605-115 states oral permission for absence may not be granted at beginning or termination of ordinary leave. 4. 1st Lt. James R. Downey Jr., Somerville, New Jersey vice Capt William C. Jones, 0306157, QMC, reld.

September 19, 1946: Headquarters First Army, Governors Island, and NY 4, New York. UP Ltr 210.2/1607 (12 February 46) GNGAP, Hq AGF, subject: Promotion of Commissioned Personnel, dated 12 February 1946, announcement is made of the temp promotion of fol named first lieutenants to the grade of Capt in AUS. With rank fr date of this order. James R. Downey Jr. 0498385 CMP.

October 14, 1946 Belle Mead General Depot, United States Army, Belle Mead, New Jersey. 4. Fol officers are hereby reld 4214th ASU and reasgd 1308 ASU eff 1 October 1946; Capt. James R. Downey Jr., 0498385 CMP.

1946 Form 1040 Total: $1948.00.

March 31, 1947: War Department Certificate of Training as satisfactorily completed training in Course C Leadership and Command Responsibilities, Course D Administration, and Course E Personnel Management.

April 4, 1947: Belle Mead General Depot, United States Army, Belle Mead, New Jersey. Ord lv of absence for twenty-three (23) days eff 0/a 5 April 1947 granted Capt. James R. Downey Jr., 0498385, CMP. Par 20 AR 600-115 dtd 20 August 1946 requires Off to keep a personal record of lv used. Par 4e, AR 600-115 states oral permission for absence will not be used to extend a lv period.

May 26, 1947: Headquarters First Army Governors Island, NY 4 New York. Aub. Appointment under Section 37 National Defense Act, as amended. To: Capt. James Richard Downey Jr. 0-498385, MP-Res 1308 ASU Belle Mead General Sub-Depot, Belle Mead, New Jersey. 1. The Secretary of War has directed me to inform you that by direction of the President, you are tendered appointment in the Officers Reserve Corps, Army of the United States effective this date, in the grade, section, and with serial number shown in address above, for a period of five (5) years.

August 26, 1947: Belle Mead general Depot, United States Army, Belle Mead, New Jersey 1. Ord lv of absence for five (5) days off o/a 29 August 1947 granted Capt James R Downey Jr., 0-498385, CMP. Par 20, AR 600-115 dtd 20 August 1947 requires Off to keep a personal record of lv used. Par 4e, AR 600-115 states oral permission for absence will not be used to extend a lv period.

February 11, 1948: Headquarters Tennessee Military District. 214 Stahlman Building Nashville 3 Tennessee 12. Fol off orc are reld atchd Mil Dist Pool and atchd Units indicated. BDCMR 15 February 1948; Capt Billy R Downey 01 284 681 QM-Res (EAD-AUS) Capt James R. Downey Jr. 0 498 385 MP-Res (EAD-AUS).

Note: Billy Ray Downey is one of my father's brothers. Bernard J. Downey is the other brother. All three served in the US Army.

February 12, 1948: 1308 ASU, Belle Mead General Depot, Belle Mead, New Jersey. Subject Certificate of Eligibility for Enlistment in Grade One. Reference is made to paragraph 4, TWX (WCL 28034), 4 February 1948, from Department of Army, quoted in letter Headquarters, First Army, Governors Island, New York. Subject: Enlistment in Grade one of Non-Regular Army Officers and Warrant Officers, file 342 AHFAG, dated 7 February 1948. 2. Application is made for certificate of eligibility for enlistment in Grade One. 3. The following information is submitted: a. Name: Downey James Richard Jr. b. Present Grade Captain Arm or Service CMP Army Serial Number o-498385. c. Date discharged to accept appointment as Commissioned Officer. 10 November 1942. d. RA-Enlisted man from: 29 July 1927 to 28 July 1930, 1 August 1930 to 5 August 1933. 24 October 1933 to 23 October 1936, 25 October 1936 to 10 November 1942. e. Army Serial Number as enlisted man: 6360147 f. Grade as regular army enlisted man on 1 January 1941: Sergeant (Date of appoint as Sgt: 7 December 1939).

April 15, 1948: Department of the Army; Each of the fol-named CMP officers Mos 9110 is reld fr asgmt and dy as indicated and is asgd to the European Comd, Bremerhaven, Germany, Shpmt OM-J174-CU (a). WP fr present sta to Cp Kilmer Pers Center, New Brunswick, New Jersey, reporting not later than 9 July 1948 to await call of the CG NYPE, Brooklyn, New York. When notified that transportation is available WP that port for transportation. Upon arrival at destination will report for dy re Req 686. EDCMR 9 July 1948. PCS. TPA. TDN. 901-18 P 431-02, 03,

07 A 2190425 S99-999. Almt for—Capt James R. Downey Jr. 0498385 1308th ASU Belle Mead Gen Depot, Belle Mead, New Jersey.

July 3, 1948: Port call Ft. Hamilton, Brooklyn, New York for Mrs. Downey and son.

July 17, 1948: headquarters usat General D. Sultan Office of the Transportation Commander; Letter of appreciation. I desire to express to you, and through you, to the members of the voyage staff, my sincere appreciation for the highly efficient manner in which you have performed your various duties.—Captain James R. Downey.

Postmarked April 16, 1948: War Department Office of the Provost Marshal General Washington 25, D.C. Captain James R. Downey Jr. Belle Mead General Depot Belle Mead, New Jersey. Dear Captain Downey: I desire to express my appreciation for the interest and patriotism you have demonstrated by accepting a Reserve Commission in the Corps of Military Police. During the past war, much of the success and good reputation earned by the Corps was due to the untiring efforts of the reserve officer to make the military police motto "Of the Troops and For the Troops" a reality. Experience of the United States Army in two wars has demonstrated that a well-trained and enthusiastic Reserve Corps of military police officers during peacetime is necessary to provide a strong foundation for possible mobilization in the event of war. To you falls the responsibility of maintaining the tradition of service to the command, which has so marked the Corps of Military Police in the past. You should, therefore, keep yourself informed in military police doctrine, training, and operational techniques to insure that your professional competence will not be lost. I urge you to continue your efforts to increase your professional knowledge by taking advantage of every available opportunity for active duty and extension course training. Since the success of the Military Police Reserve Officers Corps is of vital importance to the ultimate effectiveness of the Corps of Military Police, I will follow all phases of the Reserve program with great interest. If my staff or I can be of any assistance, please do not hesitate to call us. Sincerely B.M. Bryan, Brigadier General, The Provost Marshal General.

January 29, 1949: Time for the 7802 Station Compliment Unit To Hold Its Annual Company Party Featuring and Presenting As Their Guests of Honor "The Bremen Barons." Menu: Auderes Shrimp Cocktail Fruit Cup Half of Bremen Fried Chicken Mashed Potatoes w/Creamed Gravy

Frozen Green Peas Waldorf Salad Clover Leaf Rolls w/butter Olives and Relish Ice Cream and Cake Coffee Cream and Sugar. No Excuses for Burping Officers. Listed are those invited to attend with their Guests by the Enlisted Men of the 7802 Station Compliment Unit. Capt. Downey is listed.

April 29, 1949: Headquarters Bremerhaven Port of Embarkation, APO 69 US Army: up AR 600-115, and Cir 132, HQ AECIUM, 48, lv of absence is granted pers listed below. Pars will have sufficient negotiable dollar instruments with which to defray all expense incident to this t.l. outside United States occupied zones, US Army messing and billeting or other facilities are not auth, and bearer of this order will not request any Comdr. to provide such facilities. *Will pick up Holland visa at Bremen, Germany. **Will pick up Italian visa at Frankfurt, Germany. ** Capt. James R Downey Jr. 382 MP SV BN, APO 69 Twenty days (20) Holland, Belgium Luxembourg, France, Italy, and Switzerland.

August 26, 1949: Headquarters Bremerhaven Port of Embarkation, APO 69 Report of Survey No. 1657. In accordance with the provisions of par 134a, TM14-904 notification is hereby given of the final action taken on subject Report of Survey Property: Accountable or Responsible Officer: Capt. James R. Downey Jr. Date Initiated: 4 April 1949. First Item: Tent, command post, M-1942 $196.22. Final Action: Date 19 August 1949. All concerned are relieved of pecuniary liability, responsibility, and/or accountability.

October 19, 1949: Mrs. Thisbe C. Downey, 82 Kurfuersten Allee, Bremen Germany.

Nov 9, 1949: Lv 15 days to Berchtesgaden Germany 382 MP Sv Bn APO 69.

Dec 9, 1949: United States Senate. Re: Army Capt. James R. Downey Jr. RA-18256543 Attached letter to Pfc. Floyd J. Courtade Company D 382nd MP Bn., APO 751. Honorable Russell B. Long, United States Senate response from Col. Blakeney to the Senator. I am replying further to your letter of November 21, 1949, expressing your interest in a communication you received from Private first class Floyd J. Courtade, Company D. 382nd Military Police Service Battalion, APO 69, c/o Postmaster, New York, in which he protests the reassignment of his company commander, Capt. James R. Downey Jr. The army is glad to have the comments of Private Courtade; however, an investigation shows that Captain Downey was relieved of that assignment for cause due to the fact he had failed to carry out necessary orders and the fact that the Command Inspection conducted by the Commanding General and his staff, of which Captain Downey had knowledge for several weeks prior to such inspection, revealed that his company was completely unsatisfactory. Further, many of the unsatisfactory conditions existed and were reported on numerous inspections prior to the inspection concerned. The loyalty of the enlisted men of this company, as expressed by Private Courtade, is commendable, and their interest in efficient operation of the army is appreciated. I sincerely regret my reply could not be more favorable.

January 2014. E-mail from Floyd J. Courtade: "As indicated above he paid for the tent. When he assumed command, the GP Tent was inventoried as such; in reality it was just a large piece of canvas. So much for honesty." My response: "Thanks for remembering. As a retired TSG, I figured he was set up for something: letter and orders before and after those dates do not agree with the 'unsatisfactory' remark." I was ten years old then, but I was aware how much the men liked him—the reason being he came up through the ranks, joined the army in 1927 at the age of sixteen to break horses, and was in China in 1933 when Japan started with China. Went from horses to motorcycles. I do remember him taking me for a ride on a motorcycle down the autobahn. And my mom giving him *what for.*

December 23, 1949: Headquarters Bremenhaven, Port of Embarkation, Above off Wp o/a 23 December 1949 fr present sts to Herford, Germany (British Zone) on TDY for a period not to exceed one (1) day for the purpose of Sp Courier and upon compl of such TDY will rtn to proper sta. TCNT.

January 9, 1950: Headquarters Bremerhaven Port of Embarkation, APO 69 US Army Special Orders Number 6: 1. Capt James Richard Downey Jr. 0498385 CMP 382 MP Svc Bn APO 69 is reld fr present asgmt and dy and trfd 7834 Ord Dep Det APO 757 Griesheim Germany. Off will comply with Cir 53 Hq EUCOM 47 as amended prior to departure fr this comd. Off and dependents will comply with cir 22 Hq EUCOM 48 prior to departure fr this comd. TCNT. Tvl by Govt rail T is dir, TPA fr present sta to new dy sta is auth at no expense to the Govt.TDN. 2100425 001-218 P431-02 03 S99-999. Cost of T within Germany is chargeable to 2100425-G 1-2 GP432-02 S99-999. (Auth: Message Form#4754 dtd 3 January 1950.) Dependents: Thisbe Downey (wife) James R. Downey III (son) (PCS) EDCMR 16 January 1950.

January 16, 1950: Army Extension Courses, The Military Police School, Camp Gordon, Georgia to Commanding Officer Company D. 382nd MP Sv Bn Apo 60 US Army, C/C Postmaster New York, New York 1. Transmitted herewith is the Notice of Completion of Subcourse 40-4 of the Army Extension Courses, The Military Police School.

March 2, 1950: Restricted Headquarters Grisheim Ordnance Depot APO 757 US Army To Capt James R. Downey Jr., 0498385 7833rd Ordnance Depot Company APO 757, US Army, 1. Above named officer detailed TDY five (5) days, 6 through 10 March 1950, at Kitzingen Training Center, Kitzingen, Germany, for the purpose of attending Class 3 instructor's course for Atomic Energy Indoctrination Program (Phase II of the Department of Army Atomic Information Program). Upon completion of this duty, officer will return to proper station.

May 23, 1950: Headquarters Griesheim Ordnance Depot, APO 757, US Army; Capt James R. Downey Jr., 0489385, 7834 Ord Depot Dey, Apo 757. Above named officer and EM detailed TDY four (4) days to attend two (2) days course of instruction in Ordnance technical matters scheduled to be given at Bamburg Ammunition Depot, Bamburg, Germany, June 1 and 2 1950. Above personnel will report to CO, Bamburg Ammunition Depot during daylight hours 31 May 1950. Upon completion of this duty, personnel will return to proper station.

August 31, 1950: @. A special court martial is appointed to meet at HQ Griesheim Ordnance Depot, APO757, US Army on 6 September 1950, or as soon thereafter as practicable, for the trial of such persons as may be brought before it. Capt. James R. Downey 0-489385 7834th Ord Depot Det.

December 21, 1950: Headquarters Frankfurt Military Post APO 757 US Army. 5. The fol off are rol fr asg 7834 Ord Depot Det and asg 7835 Sandhofon Ord Automotive Ctr Dot APO 403-A. EDCMR: 1 January 1951. Mvmt of dependents will be in compliance w/provisions of BUCOM Cir 22 50. TDN. Cost of rail trans (pers) is chargeable to 2112409-G 89-1022 G461-02 S91-506. Cost of mvmt of HHG is chargeable to 2112409-G 89-1022 G425-03 S910-506. WP PCS. Auth: Ltr Hq USAREUR C/ORD subj: Reassignment of off 8 Dec 50 AG 210.3 AG Capt. James R. Downey Jr. 0498385 MPC.

December 31, 1950: It is hereby certified that Capt. and Mrs. J. R. Downey have always been charming guests at the Stork Club and that they are welcome anytime. The Chief Stork rep. Charlie the Bartender Bremen: New Tear, 1950.

August 2, 1951: Headquarter 7835 Sandhofen Ordnance Automotive Center Detachment, APO 403-A: The following named Off & EM are reld fr asgd 7835 Sandhofen Ord Autmv Cen Det, APO 403-A, US Army, and asgd in gr to 7841 Ord Proc Det, APO 403-a U S Army. PCS. No t.l. involved. EDCMR 2 August 51, AUTH: VO OCO P&T Br.Off & EM will remain on their current dy asgmt until completion of phase out of the Sandhofen Ord Autmv Cen or unless sooner reld. (1 of 8) Capt James R. Downey Jr. 01557291 PMOS 9110.

November 7, 1951: Department of the Army Certificate of Training, This is to certify that Captain James R. Downey Ord C has satisfactorily completed the course of Military Law and the Administration of Military Justice given at Headquarters, Heidelberg Military Post, APO 403, US Army.

November 17, 1951: headquarters Heidelberg Military Post, APO 403, US Army. Subject: Alert for Movement to Zone of Interior on Permanent Change of Station. To: Capt. James R. Downey Jr. 0498385, 7841 Ordnance Proc Gp, Apo 403-A. 1. You are hereby alerted for movement on or about 4 January 1952 from your present station to the BPOE, APO 69 for further movement to the Zone of Interior on a permanent change of station.

NOTE: What an education I received while on this tour in Germany, a trip up the Rhine River on Hitler's yacht. Attended the first Passion Play in Oberammergau after the war, spent a week with a school class in Holland, stayed with a Dutch family. Visit to Hitler Eagle Nest and visited the Salt mines. Visit to Switzerland. Road train into Berlin through the Russian corridor. Visited a lot of castles. Rode a bunch of cable cars. Spoke enough German to act as translator for my parents. July 1948 to December 1951.

December 19, 1951: Headquarters Heidelberg Military Post APO 403: Pac DA Cable DA-46645, dtd 24 November 1951, Capt James R. Downey Jr. 0498385 MPC MOS 9110 (Cau) is reld fr asg and dy w/7841 Ord Proc Gp

APO 403-a and is asg to 1311th ASU, Raritan Arsenal, Metuchen, New Jersey (PCS).

March 2, 1953: Headquarters Raritan Arsenal, Metuchen, New Jersey 1. Capt James R. Downey Jr., 0 498 385 385, MPC, 9359th TSU, this Ars WP o/a 2 March 1953 on TDY for approx one (1) day to USMA West Point, New York in connection with Ordnance Activities reporting upon arrival to Mr. Donald Clark. Upon compl of TDY Off will rtn to proper sta. (I wrote West Point to try and get the rest of the story, without success.)

May 8, 1953: DP announcement is made of the temporary promotion and commissioning of the fol-named offs in the Army of the United States under provisions of subsec 515 (c) of the Officer Personnel Act of 1947 in the grade and with date of rank as indicated. Capt to Major with Fr 8 May 1953, James R. Downey Jr. 0498385 MPC (USAR).

April 14, 1953: Headquarters Raritan Arsenal, Metuchen, New Jersey Special Orders No. 34. 3. The following OFF and EM 9359th TSU, this Ars WP o/a 20 April 1953 on TDY for approx five (5) days to Fort Dix, New Jersey for the purpose of participating in the first Army Special Services Bowling competition. Upon compl of TDY OFF and EM wil rtn to Raritan Arsenal. T.l. by govt. transportation auth. TDY to be performed without expense to the government. TDN 1 of 6: Capt. James R. Downey, 0 498 385, MPC.

October 1, 1953: Depart of the Army Office of the Adjutant General Washington 25 D.C. Subject Appoint as a Reserve Commissioned Officer of the army under the Armed Forces reserve Act of 1952 (PL 476, 82d Congress) (AR 135-157) Major James Richard Downey Jr., 0 498 385. By direction of the President, you are appointed as a Reserve Commissioned officer of the Army, effective this date in the grade and with service number shown in address above.

October 13, 1953: Department of the Army, Office of the Adjutant General, Washington 25, D.C. Major James R. Downey Jr., Ordnance Corps, Raritan Arsenal, Metuchen, New Jersey. The record shows that you have earned the Armed Forces Reserve Medal and/or appurtenances as follows: Medal 29 September 1942 to 28 September 1952. The period from 29 September 1952 to date has accrued toward an additional award of the medal.

1953 Form 1040: Add amounts Total: $6008.52.

1954 Form 1040: Adjusted Gross Income: $6402.24.

April 4, 1955: Requested that I be retired on 30 June 1955 after completion of more than twenty-seven years active Federal service, including more than ten years active commissioned service.

June 13, 1955: Department of the Army Washington 25, D.C., Special Orders No. 116 Extract Major James R. Downey Jr. 0498386 AUS (MAJ MPC-USAR upon his appl is ret fr active svc 30 June 1955 under prov sec 5 act Cong appr 31 July 1935 as amended by sec 3 act Cong appr 13 June 1940 sec 202 act Cong appr 29 June 1948 and act Cong appr 16 July 1953 (PL 126 Eighty-Third Cong) after more than twenty-seven yrs active Fed svc. He is rel fr asg dy, Metuchen, NJ 30 June 1955 and at proper time WP his home, Dickson, Tennessee, or the place fr which ordered to AD, Ft. Bragg, North Carolina. PCS. TDN.PHHGSIA. 2152010 501-11-211-14 P 1311-02, 03 07 S99-999.

June 27, 1955: Ordnance Corps, Raritan Arsenal, Metuchen, New Jersey. Subject: Bon Voyage to: Major James R. Downey Jr., Provost Marshal, Raritan Arsenal, Metuchen, New Jersey. Upon the occasion of your retirement from the service of the US Army after many long and faithful years, all personnel join me in recognition of your service and in wishing you the best of success for your future and a heartfelt *bon voyage*. R. E. Philips Lt. Col. Ord Corps, Commanding.

January, 1957: The following is an excerpt of an article submitted by Capt. H. M. Strassburger to the Military Police Journal, which appeared on page 15 of the January 1957 issue.

3800 Acre Beat
The Raritan Arsenal Guard Force patrols a beat comprising the 3800 acres of the Arsenal, located in Edison Township between New Brunswick and Perth Amboy, New Jersey, near the mouth of the Raritan River. The Arsenal was established as a federal reservation in 1916 and recently celebrated its fortieth anniversary. The mission of this installation is many fold and includes among other: Ordnance Corps MSS (Modern Army Supply System Depot, Home of the National Maintenance Publication Center (Ordnance), Combat Vehicle Rebuild Shops, Field

Service Division (H, K&Y Groups) and the Ordnance Corps Preventive Maintenance Agency (publishers of the well-known *PS Magazine*).

The Guard Force is commanded by Capt. H.M. Strassburger, MPC Provost Marshal, who is most capably assisted by Deputy Chief Charles W. Frye, a guard force veteran of 32 years of government service. The force is comprised of a total of 69 civilian guards, who provide security for this vast area and its nearly 3500 employees. The mission of the Guard Force is comparable to that of any police organization and includes safeguarding of the depot, its personnel and government property, the regulation and control of circulation of personnel and vehicles, the maintenance of an identification system, and the prevention of minor incidents and offenses.

The Guard Force was first established in 1918, the Arsenal having previously been guarded by military units; it had 300 men and 140 horses. Later, in 1921, the Guard Force was disbanded and elements of the 22d Infantry guarded the Arsenal. The Guard Force was again organized in 1922 and has remained an important activity of the Arsenal since, coming to a peak during the World War II years with a strength of 279 guards. A Security, Safety, and Intelligence Division was then established, the Guard Force becoming part of this division. During World War II, the Guard Force had 21 female members. In 1952, the Provost Marshal Office was established. Capt. James R. Downey, (Now Major-Retired) being the first Provost Marshal of the Arsenal, even though other MPC Officers had been assigned, he was the first appointed Provost Marshal, when the Technical Service Provost Marshal Program went into effect.

August 8, 1955 Date of Claim (FL3-39 Acknowledgment of Receipt of claim. Appears to be a VA claim form.)

References: Part 1

Personnel military file from the National Personnel Records Center, St. Louis, Missouri. Photos are from James R. Downey photo albums. Most of the contents are quotes copied from military orders.

Websites are included in contents to simplify review.

E-mail and letter correspondences from:
National Personnel Records Center, St. Louis Missouri, April 7, 2007.

Field Artillery Replacement Training Center 5th Training Regiment, Fort Bragg, 1941.

China's Trial By Fire: the Shanghai War of 1932, Donald A. Joedan, The University of Michigan Press.

PART 2

Helicopters

Chapter 1

Introduction

The year is 1994, and I finally started putting together sort of a story. It was inspired by the receipt of the questionnaire from the 366th Fighter Group Association (WWII). PO Box 392, Harrodsburg, Kentucky, 40330.

Reason

1. I was going through my father's picture albums and military papers. There are many pictures; however, I had no idea of what they were about unless notations were provided. Unfortunately, he died January 5, 1986. In 2005, I started with a simple question. Where did our paths cross? It was separate from this project.

2. I am a second- and last-generation soldier. My father quit high school and joined the army—enlisted. He broke horses and was in the last of the horse cavalries and horse-drawn artilleries. He made a horse ride from North Carolina through Louisiana prior to World War II. He was at Fort Bragg, North Carolina, when the big one broke out. At some point in time between the Philippines and France (Fort Bragg), he went from First Shirt (First Sergeant) to Second Lieutenant, ending up on a motorcycle in France. After twenty-eight years in service to this country, he retired as a major. Maybe it has taken one generation to learn, so it would not be so hard on the next generation to understand the whys of war. My wife often asks why I watch war stories. I keep telling her I am still trying to figure out the whys of war.

3. I also wanted tell this story so my children and grandchildren would have some idea of what I did on my three trips to the Vietnam War. Keep in mind that I do not consider myself any kind of war hero. I had a job to do, and I believed then that the cause was proper and just. My dad did not consider himself a hero, either. Also keep in mind that I was not a grunt (soldier on the front line) and did not wander around in the jungles of Vietnam. At the same time, it was not the safest place.

Jim Downey

Credit

I consider my wife to be the true hero. She raised two children in my absence and helped me maintain my sanity each time I returned, sometimes at a great expense to her. Without her, I would not be at this point. Names to remember: My wife, Diann Marie (Schefer) Downey; daughter, Jennifer Marie (Downey) Baldwin; granddaughters, Susan Thisbe Baldwin, Olivia Marie Baldwin; daughter, Deborah Marie Downey.

Note: Each question's response is divided into three parts based on location and time. "Danang" 1966–1967, "Udorn" 1969–1970, and "Korat/ Bien Hoa" 1972–1973.

Chapter 2
Questions 101–122

Name: James Richard Downey III
366th Rank: Staff Sergeant
Home phone: 318-443-4910
E-mail: jimdowney333@aol.com

(101) What was your job assignment?

Aircraft Pneudraulic Technician. (AFSC) 42172. (Air Force Specialty Classification).

(102) What were your duties?

Maintain both hydraulic and pneumatic systems on: F-4C aircraft while stationed at Danang, Republic of Vietnam; HH-53 aircraft while stationed at Udorn Royal Thailand Air Force Base (RTAFB); A-7D aircraft while stationed at Karat RTAFB. Troubleshoot/maintain/repair hydraulic systems on any type aircraft. Nickname was *drip* fixer. I had enlisted in the airforce after graduating from Columbia Military Academy, Columbia, Tennessee, 1958 and enlisted that same year. I re-enlisted in 1962.

(103) Did you perform any other duties?

Danang: Sergeant stuff in addition to fixing aircraft hydraulic systems.

Udorn: Green footer was a morale booster. Somehow I was selected and/ or volunteered to apply the mark of the Jolly Green Giant's green feet on the posterior of the exiting commander. This happened on the occasion of the then Squadron Commander DEROS (going home). Two of the larger PJs (Pararescue Jumper) enlisted types, the guys who leave the helicopter "Jolly" to descend to the ground and physically help the downed pilot to the hoist—should that need arise. The PJs flip a coin before the flight, and the winner gets to go down the Penetrator should the need arise. *National Geographic* printed an article in their September 1968 issue titled "Air Rescue Behind Enemy Lines" (article and photographs by Howard Sochurek, pages 346 through 369). *Fantastic reading.* I was still the new guy on the block, but my solving the tail rotor trouble was evidently appreciated. (See question #402.) I was selected from the audience to stencil—with a spray can of green paint—a green foot on each cheek of the commander's backside. The stencil was something like stenciling letters and numbers on shipping boxes, only instead of the cardboard letter cut-outs, this stencil was a cut-out of a small footprint. Note: I was not responsible for painting anything else that was hanging around between his legs. Someone of unknown origin took the spray can of green paint from me. I was amazed at the exceptionally high morale of this squadron. I had never experienced anything like it before. The mark of the Jolly Green Giant was left in a lot of different places, sometimes getting the new commander in hot water with the rest of the squadrons at Udorn RTAFB Thailand. While we were at Utapao near Bangkok, Thailand—reassembling new HH-53 on an aircraft carrier and at dockside—we took time to paint a large green foot on the side of the dock. Also, on the way out of the gate to the port, the guards' attention was distracted while the back of the guard shack was green-footed. On the ramp at Utapao, we green-footed the ramp with steps to the edge of the ramp and then painted a green puddle. This was a B-52 Base and I understand that somehow green feet appeared in the cockpit of one of the B-52s. One other time a six-foot green foot was painted on the floor of a C-130. Note: I was not the only green-footer.

Korat: Aircraft repair and temporary duty to fix an A-7D back at my old base at Udorn RTAFB and temporary duty to Bien Hoa Vietnam—and of course more sergeant stuff.

(104) Unit served with:

Danang: To: Initially assigned to the 6252 TAC. Ftr. Wg. PACAF, APO. San Francisco 96337. From: 319 Fld. Maintenance Sq., SAC. Grand Forks AFB. North Dakota. 58201. Remarks: Proceed Date, 23 March 1966. Line GV1881-PAF-Vietnam-July. Airman volunteer. Attached to 4592 Student Sq. for administration during TDY. Report at 311A Fld. Tng. Det. MacDill AFB. Charge of Quarters) NLT. 0800, 12 April 1966. Amt to be endorsed. Note: I was one of the troops who got stuck because of unknown reasons. My orders were dated 14 March 1966. I left Grand Forks 23 March 1966 and after completing F-4 school at MacDill, I waited for a port call at Orlando, Florida. I reported weekly to McCoy AFB Florida for a port call. I was finally advised (by McCoy personnel) to start to Travis Air Force Base California without a port call. At that time the airlines were on strike, so I took a hop from McCoy AFB Florida to Charleston South Carolina, then another hop (hitch hike) via C-124 to Travis AFB, California. What a trip! Because I did not have a port call, I was sent from Travis AFB to Saigon RVN on space available. Thus I flew on a Pan American civilian plane first class to Vietnam. I arrived in country 10 August 1966 and was assigned to the Thirty-Fifth FMS (Field Maintenance Squadron). Somehow during the year I was assigned to the 366th Fld. Maintenance Squadron (PACAF) APO, San Francisco, 96337. In July, I was sent to Nakhon Phanom, RTAB (Royal Thailand Air Force Base). Purpose: To make repairs on aircraft (see 311). Remarks: VOCO (verbal orders of the commander). On 4 July 1967 VOCO is confirmed, existing emergencies of the service having been such as to preclude issuance of competent written orders in advance. Member will submit travel claims for this travel no later than three (3) days after receipt of these orders. Estimated date 8 July 1967 through 11 July 1967. One thing learned on this trip was that if I had to come back to this war, Thailand was the place to be. Little did I know at that time. I was delayed five days of the 8 August 1967 DEROS (going home) so I could reenlist and save some tax money. Also I had to write my congressman in order to get my leave back. I had lost a bunch while I was waiting on my port call. I had tried all the military channels and exhausted all the air force complaint systems to include the Inspector General (IG). My request for reinstatement of my leave was denied; no one understood that it was not my fault. Finally I wrote my congressman in Tennessee and explained my problem. Thus by memorandum dated 23 January 67, I was charged no leave for the period 24 May 1966 to 5 August 1966, Docket Number 67-011. Seventy-four days of leave were returned.

Udorn: From: 3500 FLD Maint Sq. (ATC), Reese AFB Texas, 79401, To: 40 Aerospace Res/Rcy Sq. (Rescue and Recovery Squadron) (MAC), APO San Francisco 96237. Remarks: This is a *remote assignment*.
Member is M-16 qualified. Code SEA applies. Departed Reese AFB TX 2 June 1969, arrived at Udorn RTAFB 09 June 1969. Departed Udorn 5 July 1970 originally for 363 TAC Recon Wg. (TAC) Shaw AFB, SC 29152 (PAS: SPTFDX) however, while in route orders were changed to: 4472 Support Sq, Eleventh TDS, (Tactical Drone Squadron) TAC (Tactical Air

Command) Davis Monthon AFB, and Arizona. 85707 (PAS: DFTRO2). I was probably responsible for the change, as I really did not want to go to Shaw AFB. I had written a pretty strong letter to my sponsor at Shaw, and felt he probably notified the commander, resulting in a change of orders. Possibly someone was watching after me again, as the 4472nd was another small, high-morale squadron with a unique job, Tactical Drones. Two C-130s, which carried four each.

On the second trip's flight from San Francisco, a young soldier tried to open the emergency hatch over the wing of the commercial airplane. This happened about halfway between California and Hawaii. We changed the seating arrangement so that two rather large dudes sat on each side of him. Needless to say, many different kinds of cops were waiting on him when we landed in Hawaii, both military and civilian. We all figured that this young soldier had a problem with fear—about Vietnam and death; he just lost control and wanted out.

Korat: From: England AFB, LA. To: Myrtle Beach AFB, South Carolina. Purpose of TDY (temporary duty assignment) JCS. Directed Deployment. Plan ID 9950A Return to: England AFB, Louisiana. Even though the TDY indicated Myrtle Beach, we went the other direction. Remarks: Temporary Duty Folder will be hand carried. OJT Records will be hand carried by airman in upgrade training. An issue of hand tools will be hand carried by authorized personnel. A minimum of three sets of fatigues and two pairs of boots and/or wing walker shoes are required. Loading Crew Personnel will deploy with loading crew toolboxes and crew records. Thirty days advance per diem authorized. Endorsed travel orders will be issued. Travel by military air directed when available. Travel vouchers will be submitted to Accounting and Finance Office within five working days after completion of travel. Travelers will verify availability of organic military air with designated OPR/Comdr. prior to departure from TDY stn. (station) DD Form 1351-5 must be obtained at TDY location if quarters and/or meals are not available or are considered impractical to use. This deployment constitutes deployment with unit of attachment. This was an A-7 deployment, and we were to assist "The Sons of the Beaches." Left England AFB, Louisiana 15 October 1972 and returned 16 January 1973.

When we landed in Hawaii, an interesting thing happened.

Understand we were on our way to Korat, not returning. Everyone looked down in the face. We had just left wives and family about ten hours earlier. For some of us it was the first trip; for others it was the second or third trip. We were coming down the large corridor at the civilian airport in Hawaii. The waiting areas were on each side, and they were full of travelers. All of those people—and I mean all—stood up and cheered and applauded us. I can still feel the chills. Everyone, who just prior to that had been dragging their feet, now had a smile and a straight body, shoulders back. That one incident made up for some of the negatives of my previous trips when there had been name calling and accidental body contact at the civilian airport in California. It did not occur anywhere else in the country, to me. I sent the story to *Reader's Digest*, but I never heard anything back.

(105) What was the unit's insignia?

Danang: Nothing when I first arrived, but at some point the 366 became known as the "Gunfighters." I do have both a patch and photos. The patch is a phantom with a Gatling gun.

Udorn: The Super Jolly Green Giant. The patch was the Jolly Green Giant, and it was both approved and supported by the Jolly Green Giant Vegetable Co. Being the Super Jolly, our Giant had a cape. Our trademark was green feet, which were stenciled everywhere (photos).

Korat: There was an A-7D patch, and based on the stories heard from the FACs (Forward Air Controllers), "The Big D" was quite the bombing platform. Story goes of a FAC controlling one of the first air strikes involving the "D."

If you asked them to hit his smoke, they would. *Putting out the smoke or hit my smoke* meant that the forward air controllers would mark targets with smoke for other aircraft to hit. Most of the time no one actually hit the smoke. However the Big "D" could—and did. There was also a story about the FACs being accustomed to a saturation strike by F-4s. They could not understand when a "D" pilot asked for a specific target—such as which building in the cluster the FAC wanted destroyed—and the FAC, thinking he was joking, asked him to take out the one with the rusty roof, which he did on the first pass. The Big "D" was also used as SANDY, in support of rescues, as they were running out of A-1Es. Referring again to the lead article in *National Geographic*: "They are called Jolly Green Giants and Big Ugly Fat Fellows, and when they hover above North

Vietnam's perilous ocean of jungle, life hangs in the balance. They are watched over by Sandys and succored by Crowns. Inside them ride men called PJs and others wearing King Arthurs—and they are among the bravest and most selfless men I have ever known."

(106) Which of the 366 bases were you stationed at, and what were the dates?

Danang: 366th Fld Maint Sq. (PACAF) APO San Francisco 96337, Danang RVN. From 15 August 1966 to 13 August 1966. I do have photographs.

Udorn: 40th Aerospace Res/Rcy Sq. (MAC) APO San Francisco, 96237 from: 9 July 1969 to 5 July 1970. I do have photographs.

Korat: TDY with the Myrtle Beach Bunch to Korat. Arrived Korat RTAFB Thailand 17 October 1972, departed 16 January 1973 back to England AFB, Louisiana. I do have photographs.

(107) What kind of runways did they have?

Danang: Concrete/blacktop. Also old French revetments were in place when I first arrived. The revetments consisted of local sand and concrete (photos). However, during a rocket attack that year—which destroyed some of them—they were starting to be replaced with metal revetments filled with dirt. When I returned in 1969, they had also constructed hard shell revetments/concrete—covered.

Udorn: Black top.

Korat: Black top.

(108) Which was your favorite base?

England AFB in Alexandria, Louisiana, was my favorite base of all the bases I was stationed at during my twenty years. Why? It was the closest thing to country air force. Of the three bases above, Udorn was my favorite, because the Air Rescue unit was the best managed and had the highest morale of any squadron I ever worked with. In today's terminology, it would be a good example of Total Quality Management (TQM). The term then was "shit hot." Everyone helped everyone else. Rank was not a typical barrier, and problems could easily be resolved. Even though there were a few of us specialists in the squadron, we helped the crews do anything that needed doing—and at the same time they would help us when we needed it. Pride was a big factor. Even we specialists felt we owned part of each chopper. When the Russian Mig shot down a Jolly, the crew chief not only cried because he lost his bird, but his crew cried too. Everyone took a lot of pride in his bird (helicopter).

(109) Which was your least liked base?

Grand Forks AFB in North Dakota. Too darn cold. At the Danang AFB RVN, someone was trying to kill me with regularity. However, it was a life experience and education that I have since come to appreciate. By *appreciate*, I mean that the experience gave me a different outlook on life. Things I thought were important were not that important anymore. Udorn had its times, especially when we would "cross the fence" into Laos, but as "tricky Dick" (President Nixon) said, "There are no combat troops there." Korat was also nice, mainly because no one was shooting at you and we knew it was only a TDY, except for the three rocket attacks while on the TDY to Bien Hoa RVN. Bien Hoa was a quick turnaround for the "A7D," gas, bombs, and bullets back in Vietnam.

(110) What type of shelter did you have at each base and how many shared it?

The same model tent my dad used thirty-nine years earlier.

Danang: When I arrived at Danang I stayed in an eight-man, dirt/wood-pallet floor tent with an accompanying leaking top. Shortly thereafter, I moved into a hard shell eight-man tent (*hard shell* being a solid wood floor/wood frame with a tent on top that did not leak). Each individual had a locker and cot with mosquito netting. Netting was not for mosquitoes but to keep the big rats from jumping in bed with you at night. Outside each tent was a shallow foxhole with sand bags for rocket attacks or whatever. We were not issued a weapon. About halfway into the tour I moved into the top floor of a two-story barracks constructed of wood. The outside walls were constructed of slanted one-by-six wood slats halfway up and screened. I hope a lesson was learned from that mistake, because when you put too many people in the same location—and that location is subject to rocket attack—your losses are also proportionally increased.

Udorn: Upon arrival, I spent two days downtown in a leased hotel. Then I went to a small single-story barracks and then to a two-story barracks.

Karat: Old army officers' quarters, single story, one person per room. There was a swimming pool and snack bar across the street.

(111) What was used to heat your shelter at each base?

Danang, Udorn, Korat: sunshine and wind. Needless to say there was no heat or air-conditioning.

(112) What was used to cool your shelter at each base?

Danang, Udorn, Korat: wind.

(113) What type of latrine, shaving, and shower accommodations did you have at each base? Was there running water?

Left is a fifty-holer outhouse, twenty-five each side and showers through the middle. Hot water if sun shone on the tanks. Right is a four-holer. A third of a fifty-five gallon drum used under each hole. Drums were removed daily and burned using jet fuel.

Danang: Gang shower for the then "Camp Danang": a metal shed with showerheads in the ceiling, hot water in the daytime if the sun shone on the large water drum on stilts and you were not late. The shower had runway plates for a floor, and while you were taking a shower, *mama-san* would be next to you washing clothes. Four-holer latrines (photo) with parts of a fifty-five gallon drum for waste. Same thing here—you would be doing your thing and along would come mama-san and she would squat on the hole next to you; so much for modesty. Airmen were assigned to burn the contents of the drums daily by pouring in JP4 (jet fuel) and setting fire to it (photos). Later, a fifty-hole outhouse (twenty-five holes down each side) with shower stalls in the middle was constructed (photo above). This one was flushed every four or five hours by dumping a fifty-five gallon drum of water at one end and flushing the waste out the other. Hot water was still by sunshine. After I moved into the barracks, separate bath facilities were constructed with shower stalls, sinks, and genuine flush-em-up toilets. Progress had come to Camp Danang. A urinal was constructed by digging a hole, filling it with rock, sticking a large pipe in it, and covering it back up with dirt (photo).

Udorn: Separate bathhouses shared between barracks.

Korat: Just like the real world.

(114) What kind of artificial lighting did you have at each base?

Danang: No electricity in the dirt floor tent, thus requiring a flashlight. The hard shell tent had an electrical light in the middle of the tent. The two-story barracks had one double outlet for each cubicle. Diesel-powered generators furnished the power.

Udorn: One outlet per cubicle.

Korat: Just like home.

(115) What did you sleep on/in at each base?

Danang: Stacked cots with netting in the tents and the same in the barracks, but the mosquito netting was not used. Instead of mosquito net being used against the mosquitos, it was used to keep rats from jumping on you. A picture of the rats made the news stateside.

Udorn: Single part of a bunk bed with flat springs.

Korat: Same.

(116) Did you add any improvements to provide more comfort?

Danang: After moving into the barracks, we put light bulbs under big food cans in the lockers to eliminate the mildew. One dude across the hall had his family send him a small air-conditioner, and he put plastic around his bed and the a/c blew cool air into it. He was on the bottom bunk. Sometimes you could look over and see frost on the plastic.

Udorn, Korat: No.

(117) What kind of mess facilities did you have at each base?

Chow hall, Camp Danang. Best "triple A" restaurant in the area.

Danang: Started with a field kitchen in a shed. Used a mess kit we carried to the kitchen area, ate, then washed and took back to the tent. If you suffered the "GI's" it was your own fault. After the barracks, a new mess hall was constructed. Because of the twelve-hour shift we would eat two breakfasts (one in the morning and one at midnight). The other compound held the theater and the NCO club, about a three-mile walk. Keep in mind the town of Danang was off limits. I did get to make one trip into town as part of a tour (photos).

Udorn, Korat: Regular dining facilities.

(118) What kind of "rations" did you have at each base?

Danang: If things were real busy on the flight line we would eat "C" rations. The favorite was beans and weenies.

Udorn, Korat: Dining hall food.

(119) Did you cook food/snacks in your living area?

Danang: No. However, when I first arrived we would grill steaks obtained by swapping items with the Seabees. We used charcoal found locally and pits made in the welding shop. Our area was the flight line behind the old French revetments.

Udorn: At the squadron work area we would have cookouts similar to the cookouts at Danang. That food was exceptional (photos).

Korat: Nothing.

(120) What did you "cook" on?

Danang: Grill in the shop area was a fifty-five gallon drum cut in half; charcoal was obtained from locals, and steaks from the Seabees.

Udorn: While we were putting together the new helicopters at Sattahip, the folks on the carrier gave us a four-foot X4 foot box of frozen food and we had a feast.

Korat: N/A.

(121) What foods were sent from home?

Danang: Packages received from home mainly contained chocolate chip cookies. The first package was sent regular mail and when I opened it, it was full of ants. Thereafter, packages were sent air mail.

Udorn, Korat: Cookies, mostly chocolate chip.

Danang, Udorn, Korat: Cold milk, real bread, and just plain home cooking. One of the first foods I had when I returned was a banana sandwich and a big glass of cold milk. One of the things I learned to hate was Kool-Aid.

It seems like everyone sent Kool-Aid in letters. I think it was a sales gimmick by the manufacturers of Kool-Aid. I still do not like it, and it is not allowed in my house except when the grandkids drink it. It is sorta like my father not allowing Spam in the house.

(122) Did you "barter" for "non-G.I." food and beverages locally?

Danang: Booze, lockers, and beds were bartered to the navy Seabees and the marines for steaks and strawberries.

Udorn, Korat: N/A.

Chapter 3
Questions 123–143

(123) What "G.I. food" did you dislike the most?

Danang: Eggs at breakfast were probably my favorite, mainly because we worked twelve-hour shifts most of the time. Noon to midnight was our shift; thus, we ate two breakfasts—one at midnight and one in the morning. The biggest turnoff was powdered eggs. That stuff had to be a concoction of the enemy. We could smell it two blocks from the chow hall. When that happened I would switch to SOS (ground beef/gravy on toast); my father used the term *shit on a shingle.*

Udorn: On this trip, I ate quite a bit on the Thai economy. The food was very good, and one of my favorites was fried rice. It was served on a banana leaf and cost about ten cents. I am not too picky when it comes to food, so I had no problems with the food either in the dining hall or in town. Another favorite was a trip to a local hotel restaurant that served Kobe steaks—talk about good. You could eat steak for the same price as Burger King stateside. On one of the trips into Laos (Long Tieng: "the most secret place on Earth"), I remember eating what I thought was a turkey sandwich, but I do not remember seeing one turkey my entire stay. I did see some big lizards, though. My theory about food was that if it tasted good, I would eat it and not ask questions.

Korat: The food at Korat was about the same as Udorn. No problems.

(124) Which of the following were available and on which bases?

Movies:

Danang: The main cantonment area had an air-conditioned theater. When we would get off work at midnight we would go eat breakfast, then to the movie if it was good. In one of the pictures you will notice a bunch of guys standing outside looking at the side of a barracks. What they were really doing was watching a stag film in reverse. The guys in the barracks had hung a sheet and were watching from inside the barracks, not realizing that a crowd had assembled outside that was also watching.

Korat, Udorn: I did not go to the movies much.

Clubs:

Danang: (officers or enlisted) The NCO club was a retreat and located in the old cantonment area. The then "Camp Danang" or "Tent City" only had tents and a field kitchen. Later in the year there was a mobile hospital and air-conditioned portable boxes (something like a trailer) for pilots to sleep. There was a chow hall, special services club, and laundry, which were located in Tent City. After returning in 1969, (photo) Camp Danang (Tent City) was now called "Gunfighter Village."

Udorn: Used the NCO club for drinks and entertainment.

There was a particular bar in Udorn that the squadron adopted.

Korat: The NCO club was also used here quite a bit. Also one of the military Catholic fathers set up a local pizza place and used the profits for local children.

A PX:

Danang: In the air force it was called a BX (Base Exchange). The strangest part about the Air Force BX was that it was located outside the front gate. The air force helped the indigenous personnel by hiring them to clean the tents, wash clothes, iron, shine shoes, and ask everyone "GI, you buy me BX?"

Udorn/Korat: Located on the base and provided all the necessities.

What was your favorite item? Define item.

What the TV series China Beach *was about.*

Danang: One of my favorite retreats was a trip to China Beach. I guess I got to visit it five or six times during the tour. You could actually order a hamburger that came pretty close to the real thing, except that the buns usually had extra protein (bugs) included. I was always amazed that a country with such beautiful beaches could be at war—correction, "at conflict." Much later, the TV series *China Beach* was a favorite. Strange, not a bikini in sight.

Udorn: Eating, off the base.

What did they serve?

Danang/Udorn/Korat: Drinks, some food, and entertainment.

Korat: On the TDY from Korat back into Vietnam (Bien Hoa) the war games were winding down, and so the Officers' and NCO clubs were combined (photos).

A Red Cross Unit:

Danang: At some point during the year when the service club was located in Camp Danang, the Red Cross appeared. Also, they brought a library of which I availed myself. The way I would pick a book was to pick the thickest. The Red Cross also served hot dogs. Sometimes that is what I would have for brunch, keeping in mind that most of the time we did not get to bed till 3 a.m. Someone has probably told of the story about a GI receiving a Red Cross bag full of whiskey. Fact is, it was not just a story because the dude in the next cubicle was the one, and I witnessed it. Someone stateside knew how to make one GI dude happy.

I did get to visit the town as part of a tour. Danang was normally off limits. Temples, orphanages run by the Catholic Church, a train station with a train that could not be used, gas stations, and street vendors—the town was the same as stateside, except different.

Udorn/Korat: Except for the Christmas bags, I do not remember that much involvement by the Red Cross in Thailand.

(125) Did you use V-mail or letters to communicate home?

Danang: The mail was free from in-country. Not only were letters written, but also a lot of correspondence included reel-to-reel tape recordings. I would start a tape and it would maybe take a week to fill it. I sent tapes to my wife, kids, and parents. Once, I mailed my wife Dee a small negligee in one of the tape plastic boxes, 3/4 x 6 x 4 inches. Needless to say, it was a very skimpy negligee. Before I left state side, we (Dee) became involved in the then new hobby of Citizen Band Radio (CB). While at Danang, I bought postcards of Vietnam, and with a rubber stamp I made them into CB call cards. I would mail them to CBers who would send me their cards, maybe a hundred total. The University of Memphis would send GIs the Tennessee state flag if you wrote and asked for one, and I did. The flag went on all three trips (photo). Cousin Bill Vinson visited from Ankie RVN where he was stationed with the United States Army First Calvary—helicopters, not horses.

Udorn/Korat: Used small tapes here and free mail.

(126) Were you able to phone home from overseas?

Danang: I only called home once from there, though I remember trying more than once. Calls were made via "MARS" (Military Air Radio Station). When you finished talking, you had to say "over," so the radio operator knew when to switch from transmit to receive.

Udorn/Korat: It was too expensive to call home from Udorn. However, I did call home once from Korat.

(127) Were you married before?

Danang/Udorn/Korat: I was married and had two little girls (Jennifer Marie and Deborah Marie) before being sent to Vietnam. I was into my second hitch. A hitch is a four-year tour with the air force. A bad memory that comes to mind is that after I returned, I learned how tough it had been on the kids. It seems that when other kids in school learned that I was in Vietnam, they told my girls that they would never see me again because I would be killed. Diann (Dee) and I were married November 14, 1959. I had enlisted October 10, 1958. (Note: We celebrated fifty-four years in 2014.)

(128) Did you marry one of the girls you met or corresponded with while with the 366? N/A.

(129) Did you go on leave while overseas?

Danang: I was supposed to get an R&R (rest and recuperation) while there, but because I did not have that much money, I took the week and hopped around in country. By *hopped*, I mean you show up at the airfield and put your name on a list, and you're on the next flight going your way—thus away you go, and it is called a hop. I visited my cousin, Bill Vinson, at Ankie RVN. He was a side gunner on a Chinook helicopter. The day I landed there, there was an Air Force C-130 that had run off the end of the runway at an army base. Seems it landed a bit long. Being the only air force dude there, it was just a bit embarrassing (photos).

Udorn: Again I could not afford a trip, so I took a week and stayed in a hotel.

Korat: This was a TDY, so no R&R.

(130) What sports or activities did you get involved with?

Danang: Drinking was about the only sport available to get involved in. There just wasn't time, especially with the twelve-hour shifts. I guess you could call dodging rockets a sport, and that happened regularly. At a later point in time, I called those rocket attack sports something similar to Russian roulette while playing musical chairs because of the random selection of victims.

Udorn/Korat: N/A.

(131) Did you attend any schools or take any lessons for college credit while with the 366?

Danang: Not then. I used the little extra time I had for reading books from the service club. However, prior to going to Vietnam, I had started taking correspondence courses through the air force. After retiring, I did take advantage of the GI Bill and obtained a BA in General Studies by going to night school while working. The transcript looked like a travel guide. In 1992, I completed my master's degree in Management. That happened just before England AFB, Louisiana closed. I lacked three hours in meeting the requirements for another in (HRD) Human Recourses Development. The thing that set me on the education track was while I was stationed in Grand Forks, North Dakota, and while in the tail section of a B-52 changing a hydraulic power package for the electronic troubleshooters. I was freezing my buns off, and then someone blocked my light. I said something about busting my balls changing something that was not broken—all because some electronic genius said so. As soon as I got through telling the dummy to get out of my light, I noticed something sparkling on that person's shoulder. Turns out it was a bird colonel, and he suggested I do something about my education so I to could tell people to change things themselves. I did something. I enrolled in correspondence courses offered by the air force. Then after the first tour, and while stationed at Lubbock, Texas, my kids came home from school with this stuff called "the New Math." So I enrolled in a night school at Texas Tech, thus my first college courses. Then when time permitted, I enrolled in night college courses. Before retiring, I had accumulated nearly two years' worth of college courses. I lost maybe eight courses because of temporary duty relocations (TDY). Halfway through a course I would be sent to another air force base for a short period of time, part of the job. All courses were accelerated, and if you missed just one three-hour night class, it was impossible to catch up.

Udorn/Korat: N/A.

(132) Did you receive any medical or dental treatment while with the 366?

Danang: The only thing medical that happened was that when I was changing a horizontal stabilizer control unit by myself, I hurt my back while trying to hold it in place with one hand while putting in the mounting bolts with the other hand. That little incident still brings me to my knees every now and then. I was young and stupid, or I would have sought some help. Luck was usually with me, and on numerous occasions during the rocket attacks I would not be in the wrong place at the right time. Examples: When we would get off at midnight, eat breakfast, then catch a bus back to the tent, we would usually wait at the same spot repeatedly. However this one night we decided to walk back. That night the place we usually waited took a direct hit (photos). Another time, while in bed asleep, a rocket attack knocked me out of bed. I found a piece of scrap metal within six inches of where I lay. When I first arrived, I had taken those damn malaria pills, and one night—when I was usually supposed to be at work—I was sick. Four guys jumped into a conex box that took a direct hit (photo). I would most probably have been somewhere in the area of the direct hit if not in the conex box too. A conex box is a large metal shipping container about 12x12x18 feet. One of the guys survived, but he only had part of one limb (arm) left. The squadron had a cookout to raise money for his family. That is the point where I started not remembering names.

(132A) In 1973, I had the first of two collapsed lungs. It happened while on leave and at a CB (Citizen Band Radio) convention in St. Louis. I thought I was having a heart attack. It happened again about two years later. I do not know why it happened, but I do know that I worked on Ranch Hands (C-123) at Danang, and that at least three or four times I had the stuff they sprayed (Agent Orange) all over me because the hoses used on the spray system of the Ranch Hands (C123s) usually had fluid left in them. These guys were usually shot up pretty bad because they flew low and slow. There were no deluge showers unless it was raining. Talk about leaving a bad taste; just mention the Veterans Administration. When I retired, I went to the Shreveport, Louisiana, VA hospital and they evaluated me, awarding me a 50 percent disability. About a year later, I was reevaluated by the Alexandria/Pineville VA Hospital in Louisiana. My disability was reduced to 10 percent. Part of the reason it was reduced is that I said no to being admitted to the Pineville VA Hospital. I said no because they were able to do the first assessment in one day. When I called the New Orleans VA, they threatened to discontinue my disability payments. After a few profanities and words about his lack of knowledge of who his father was and his mother's position under the porch, I advised the young dude that it was no big deal because the disability pay was subtracted from my retirement pay. The only benefit I received was the untaxed sixty dollars a month. It is the same stupid VA system that did a number on the Desert Storm troops. The best thing that could be done would be to close the entire VA Hospital system and put that money into civilian hospitals. Then give free medical to all military. As time moved on, my medical problems increased: skin cancer, colon cancer, prostate cancer, high blood pressure, diabetes, COPD, and more. Many years later the disability pay was increased. I credit a few civilian doctors with saving my life and God for putting on extra angels to help watch over me.

Jim Downey

Udorn/Korat: Just burns and scrapes.

(133) What decorations, awards, or commendations did you receive?

Danang: Standard ribbons this trip that did not amount to much, just the same ones that everyone else received. Strange though, that most everyone received a commendation medal for just showing up, except some of us. Probably because of a lazy supervisor who forgot to fill out the paper.

Udorn: Air Force Commendation Medal, 25 October 1969.

Citation to Accompany the Award: Staff Sergeant James R. Downey III distinguished himself by outstanding achievement as a Pneudraulic Technician, Fortieth Aerospace Rescue and Recovery Squadron, Udorn Royal Thai Air Force Base, Thailand, while engaged in ground operations against an opposing armed force on 25 October 1969. On that date, Sergeant Downey voluntarily went deep into hostile held territory as a member of a maintenance team dispatched to recover an aircraft which had been forced to make an emergency landing due to battle damage. The aircraft was located at a remote airstrip, which was surrounded by belligerent forces that had the capability to overrun the airstrip at will. Continually facing the possibility of attack at any moment, Sergeant Downey, with great skill and dedication, completed the necessary repairs, which enabled the aircraft to be returned to its home station. By his prompt action and humanitarian regard for his fellow man, Sergeant Downey has reflected credit upon himself and the United States Air Force.

Air Force Commendation Medal, 8 July 1969 to 5 July 1970.

Citation to Accompany The Award: Staff Sergeant James R. Downey III distinguished himself by meritorious service as Non-Commissioned Officer in Charge, Pneudraulic Shop, Fortieth Aerospace Rescue and Recovery Squadron, Udorn Royal Thai Air Force Base, Thailand, from 8 July 1969 to 5 July 1970. During this period, Sergeant Downey's outstanding skill, superior knowledge, and display of professionalism contributed immeasurably to the successful mission accomplishment of the Fortieth Aerospace Rescue and Recovery Squadron. The distinctive accomplishment of Sergeant Downey reflects credit upon himself and the United States Air Force.

Meritorious Service Medal, 22 March 1973 to 31 October 1978.

Citation to Accompany the Award: Technical Sergeant James R. Downey III distinguished himself in the performance of outstanding service to the United States as non-commissioned Officer in Charge, Ground Safety Branch, Twenty-Third Tactical Fighter Wing, England Air Force Base, Louisiana, from 22 March 1973 to October 1978. During this period, Sergeant Downey's outstanding professional knowledge, initiative, and devotion to duty were responsible for establishing a highly commendable Ground Safety Program on England Air Force Base. Sergeant Downey is an acknowledged expert on ground safety, and his effectiveness has contributed immeasurably to the air force's overall safety program. The singularly distinctive accomplishments of Sergeant Downey culminate a distinguished career in the service of his country and reflect great credit upon himself and the United States Air Force.

Ribbons:

(1) AFLSA (Air Force Longevity Service Award) (10 Oct 62) (10 Oct 64–9 Oct 67) w3OLC w4OLC

(2) AFGCM (Air Force Good Conduct Medal) (10 Oct 58–9 Oct 64) w4OLC (10 Aug 71–9 Aug 74) w5OLC (10 Oct 73–9 Oct 76)

(3) VSM (Republic of Vietnam Campaign Medal) w/2BSS

(4) NDSM (National Defense Service Medal)

(5) RVCM (Republic of Vietnam Campaign Service Medal)

(6) AFOUA (Air Force Outstanding Unit Award) (1 July 65–31 Mar 67)

(7) AFCM (Air Force Commendation Medal) w1OLC

(8) GCM (Army) (Good Conduct Medal)

(9) PUC (Presidential Unit Citation) (23 Apr 67–1 Aug 67)

(10) MSM (Meritorious Service Medal)

(11) GDCON (Air Force Good Conduct Medal)

(12) VGCUC (Republic of Vietnam Gallanty Cross with Palms)

(13) SAEMR (Small Arms Expert Marksmanship Ribbon)

(14) State of Louisiana Honor Medal, Presented by Gov. Jindal 2010

(134) Did you improve a procedure, develop a gizmo or tool, or suggest a modification that was adopted by the 366?

Danang: 29 May 1967, Suggestion Number Dan-204-67-N, $15.00 for "Doors opening the wrong way." Jerry C. Schaaf, Captain, USAF Chief, Personal Affairs Section. Suggestion No. DAN-312-67-M, $25.00, "F$O$D" (note: FOD is foreign object damage, caused by jet engines sucking up objects causing the engine to fail), Harold L Pray, Captain, USAF Chief, Personnel Affairs Section.

Udorn: 18 March 1970 "Pressure Tester," Suggestion No. UDO-239-70 was submitted for evaluation. The equipment had already been made and was in use. This small piece of equipment was used for everything. The other suggestion was titled "Small Portable Hydraulic Servicing Unit." Only this one was on site, (Udorn) not located in Laos, for use there. This information could not be included in the suggestion because "Tricky Dick" Nixon said we were not there.

15 December 1969 "Small portable hydraulic servicing cart," UDO-167-70M (number assigned to suggestion). This unit was the predecessor to the "Pressure Tester." It was built primarily to save space and improve ease of handling. One person could carry it. The regular service cart required three people to lift it. The suggestion contained the following: "Presently when servicing the hydraulic system of the HH-53B&C aircraft, a servicing cart is required. The servicing cart takes three men to load it on an aircraft to be carried to the other aircraft needing servicing, if the aircraft is located at a remote base or field where servicing equipment is not available. I have designed and constructed a

hydraulic servicing cart that can be carried by one man. The unit can be used to service the hydraulic systems and, also with quick disconnect adapters, can be used to service the damper accumulator. This unit has a tank, which holds two gallons of hydraulic fluid, a filter that filters all fluid before entering the aircraft systems, a shut-off valve to dump pressure back to the reservoir, and a hand pump. This unit was being used very successfully due to its small size of two cubic feet." Because of its usefulness this "unit" was taken to "Lima Site 98 Laos/Long Tieng/ Cheng." Thus, I had to build another, the "pressure tester." The pressure tester included the same features with additional valves, filter, and gage (photo of pressure tester). 18 March 1970, Mobility Box.

UDO-238-70. This was a kit with three rows of drawers for parts. Handles were provided for easy movement. The contents of the kit were what made it successful. It contained a selection of hydraulic fittings and seals. This kit, along with the pressure tester, saved three (3) HH-53s. First time out into the Plain of Jars, a tubing cutter, two bulkhead unions and four tubing ends, and sleeves patched flight control tubing enabling a recovery. For this trip I was awarded a commendation medal. The second time out, caps from the box enabled a non-essential hydraulic system to be capped off, for the trip back to Udorn from a rice paddy. The third time, seals enabled the repair of a leaking fitting, caps to cap unnecessary hydraulic systems, and unions so hoses robbed from the landing gear system could bypass damaged lines. I received a check for $172.00 minus $43.00 FITW, (federal income tax withheld) 4 May 1970. No checks received for the "pressure tester." Strange that it got lost in the system? Once, when Long Tieng was overrun, the tester went missing; now it's probably in a Hanoi museum.

15 December 1969, "T" hydraulic Connector for the Utility System. UDO-166-70. (See 402 Second story about the APU.) This device enabled a hydraulic mule to be connected in parallel to the system that starts the auxiliary power unit. I received a check for $112.00 minus $28.00 for FITW—plus the pleasure of seeing everyone's face appear to see who was pumping up the APU accumulator so fast (photo).

Other suggestions submitted but disapproved: 26 December 1969, UDO-179-70M, Contamination of utility hydraulic system HH-53; 1970, UDO-306-70, Fuses for brake lines (HH-53); 15 December 1969, UDO-164-70M, Dual System failure of tail rotor, HH-53. 15 December 1969, Hydraulic cooler HH-53.

Korat: No suggestion this trip. Over the twenty years I spent in the air force, I probably submitted a hundred suggestions and was paid for maybe ten. Needless to say, I was shortchanged for some of them, especially the "pressure tester and cart" above. How much are three HH-53s worth?

(135) What was your most harrowing experience?

Danang: Being blown out of the bed and finding the scrap metal so close. Being in the right place at the right time. Not in the conex box, not waiting for the bus in the wrong place, or just plain being missed. Danang was known as "Rocket Ally." One night (dark thirty AM) I worked on a special modified C-130 with extra pylons. The problem was a hydraulic leak inside one of the engine compartments. To find it, I had to climb into the engine compartment and look for the leak while the engine was running. Where would I have run if there had been a rocket attack? Found the problem and borrowed a quick disconnect from the ground equipment folks. Made a temporary repair so the plane could return to their base. The frustrating thing about rocket attacks is you don't get to get even. It is like playing Russian roulette and musical chairs at the same time.

Udorn: Leave all forms of identification behind. Be issued M-16, a bandoleer of ammo, vest, and survival vest .38 cal, box of shells, extra radio, and flight helmet. Purpose, to recover a Jolly that was forced down in the "Plain of Jars." Out by dark or destroy the bird. Everyone was involved, including "Crown." Air Force Security set up a perimeter (five dudes with M-16s). We were casually going about our business, until someone reminded us that the puffs of smoke in the distance were not Girl Scout campfires. Needless to say, smoke then came from the tools. The mobility kit immediately paid for itself. By using a small tubing cutter, the hydraulic tubing battle damage was cut out, the system repaired, serviced, tested, and we were on our merry way, posthaste. The scary part was climbing around on top of the chopper. Talk about sniper bait. It was too hot to wear the vest. But when it was over, what a high! The second time, we went to LS 98—the most secret place in the world. I robbed a hydraulic hose from the landing gear and pinned the gear so it would not work. Replaced the bad hose and returned to base. The third time to go after one was somewhere in Laos, I think. The chopper had taken hits, and the flight controls were acting strange. The pilot had ordered everyone to bail out. After everyone had left, the area cleared and the pilot and engineer found a place to put it down in a rice paddy. We were brought in the next day for the fix or destroy. Indigenous natives came out to meet us; needless to say we hoped they were friendly. We were probably the first white people they had seen. They could not get over our round eyes and hair on our chest and arms. With both language and sign, I told them, "My papa-san was a link," meaning *my daddy was a monkey*. They laughed at that. When I say we had stepped back a century, I mean back to the flint rifle and bow and arrow days. Because those were the only weapons I saw. I was impressed with their simplicity. By that, I mean they were happy and friendly (photos).

Korat: Keeping in mind this was the third trip to the land of Russian roulette. The TDY to Thailand became a TDY back to Bien Hoa Vietnam. During the sixteen-day stay we were rocketed a few times.

(136) What was your most challenging experience?

Danang: Coping with the stupidity of the war. The first time I worked on a C-123, it had just returned from the field. It was loaded with pallets of body bags. The crew had kicked out the windows in order to breathe. It is a smell that you cannot forget, not to mention the sloshing when the pallets were being removed. Most of the time the bodies had lain at least one day in the sun before being picked up. Naturally, the wounded had priority.

Udorn/Korat: N/A

(137) What was your most rewarding experience?

Danang: My then naiveté in thinking that what I was doing was to protect the freedom of our country. Being the best in my job at doing my job. I was helping to protect my children and others. I intentionally left out the Chevy, apple pie, mom, baseball, and the American way.

Udorn: Participation in the rescue of 1st Lt. Woodrow Bergeron Jr. Possible of the Twelfth TAC Fighter Wing. The following is extracted from *Searcher*, newsletter of the Forty-First Aerospace Rescue and Recovery Wing, Vol. III, No.1 January 1970 PACAF RP 64-1.

Following is the experience as related by Lieutenant Bergeron of the Twelfth Tactical Fighter Wing. The lieutenant's F-4 rolled in on its target, and then started to climb. At five thousand feet the aircraft began to lose altitude and the aircraft plunged into a steep dive. When he ejected at one thousand feet, the windblast jarred his helmet, causing a gash over the bridge of his nose and two black eyes. Coming down, he could see enemy automatic weapons directed at him. Spotting a clearing near a riverbank, he guided himself to it. Ground fire continued as he hit the ground, shed his parachute canopy, and sped for cover in a clump of bamboo. "I could hear the enemy fire ricocheting over my head," he remembered. He found a clearing, hid under driftwood and leaves, and grabbed his survival radio. "I called up, told them who I was, where I was, and come get me." Using his radio, Lieutenant Bergeron directed the sky raiders to their targets. The A-1E dropped ordnance throughout the afternoon trying to provide cover for the incoming helicopters. But the helicopters continued to take too many hits. He was advised to "dig in" for the night. The next day: "The next day went pretty much the same," he stated, "but the enemy positions were hidden in caves and bunkers, and it took quite a bit to silence them." One try by a Jolly Green seemed to be *the* rescue. Lieutenant Bergeron raced out to a bluff, and thought the helicopter copilot had spotted him. But since the embankment was so steep, he figured the HH-3 crewman lost sight of him as he started up the incline. The helicopter was about six feet away as Lieutenant Bergeron clawed at the slope. But the ground fire got so heavy the helicopter had to pull away. "I could see the skin coming off the helicopters," he pointed out. He said if they were willing to hover and take "unbelievable" ground fire, then he was willing to stick it out. More rescue attempts were made that day, but no one could get as close as before. When darkness came, he decided to find another place to hide. At the nearby river he found a mangrove-like tree with roots exposed along the bank. *Old hideout found.* Shortly after he found his new hideout, three enemy soldiers came over the edge of the river and used automatic weapons to shoot into the area he had just left. After searching the area, the enemy left. The closest any of them got to him was fifteen feet. Lieutenant Bergeron then decided to try to swim across the nearby river, but he became exhausted when he was one-third of the way across. As he swam back, he spotted a bush similar to a rose bush without thorns. Covering himself with the bush, he lay along the riverbank. In the darkness of early morning, Lieutenant Bergeron heard a 4-F streak across the area several times. "He had the A-1s and the rescue aircraft there at dawn," Lieutenant Bergeron said. Knowing where Lieutenant Bergeron was located, the sky raider pilots knew they could hit anything but the bush. "I was calling for it all around me," he remarked. "One time they came within a foot of me on a strafing pass." *Jolly Green returns.* After the enemy was attacked for six hours, the Jolly Green crew returned. Lieutenant went out into the river and on the second try of the day was picked up. "I will never forget how it feels to have that lowering device (forest penetrator) they use wrapped around me," he exclaimed. "I knew I was part of that helicopter." Citing the efforts of the rescue team, he said, "They were there when I needed them." Lieutenant Bergeron never lost faith in the men who were determined to rescue him. "They'll get you out of there. Really. Just have a radio."

The reason I say he may have been with the Twelfth Tactical Fighter Wing is that he may have well been a member of another F-4 outfit. The article by 1st Lt. Dennis P. Beck was censored for whatever reason.

Actually, a HH-53—tail number 8284 from the Fortieth ARRS stationed at Udorn and on temporary assignment to Nakon Phanom RTAFB—rescued him. He was picked up in Laos and brought to Nakon Phanom. It was a massive effort, and with the teamwork by everyone, it happened. The 53s returned the first day truly shot to hell. One of the PJs died in that attempt. The night after the first attempt, a captain was helping hold a bucking bar to scab patch bullet holes in the bottom of the helicopter when a large amount of blood splattered onto his face. He went out back of the chopper and threw up, and then he returned to finish holding the bucking bar for the repair. Everyone was helping everyone else do anything they could in order to fix the Jollys for the next day's try. One part that surfaces in dreams every now and then is, I washed or tried to wash the blood out of the area between the deck and the bottom of the chopper. Most of the PJ's blood had settled in that area. I could not believe how much blood the human body held. (http://www.nexus.net) Date of Loss: 5 December PJ David M. Davidson. Even with the PJ's loss, everyone thought it was worth it. Somewhere I have a tape of the radio communication made from one of the Jolly's radios (photos). It makes you wonder just how far the truth is/was stretched in most of the newspaper articles and if it will be—or was—corrected.

Korat: N/A.

(138) What was your most humorous experience?

Danang: 1. One night when it was quiet and the guy in the next cubicle was writing home, I reached over and unplugged his lamp. When he reached behind his locker to check the plug, I grabbed his arm, and all hell broke loose. 2. Getting into trouble for my corrective action to any problem noted in the aircraft forms. All aircraft repairs are written in the aircraft forms. A pilot had written, "Canopy hard to operate, biceps muscles of CPO required to operate." My corrective action: "Cleaned and lubricated latches with finger muscles, op's check okay, no muscles needed." Needless to say, I received counseling. 3. The next fun thing that occurred: It was approximately nine o'clock dark (2100) with rain. I was dispatched to troubleshoot an aircraft (F4) with a hydraulic problem. A hydraulic mule was delivered to the aircraft. A hydraulic mule is a power unit to operate the aircraft hydraulic without having to run the aircraft engines. The mule was low on hydraulic fluid, so I requested that it be taken back for service. Some smartass line chief told me to do it myself, and he had two cases of quart cans delivered. I tried to explain the problem of servicing a hydraulic mule with quart cans "in the rain." But the line chief did not want to hear it. I promptly serviced the mule with the quart cans provided, in the rain. Then I red X'ed the mule for suspected water contamination. When either equipment on aircraft or the aircraft itself is used, something red X'ed requires two signatures to indicate the problem has been properly repaired and tested. Note: water in the aircraft hydraulic systems is not considered to be in safe condition. Needless to say, I received an ass chewing, and after I explained the problem to the

Chief of Maintenance (an officer with more horse power than the line chief), it went away.

Udorn: Green-footing the outgoing commander's backside. A champagne helicopter flight. Native reaction to this green-eyed, white, hairy dude getting a helicopter out of their rice paddy (see 135).

Korat: One of the not-so-busy nights, we built a mortar tube out of beer cans. Take four standard-sized beer cans. Cut top and bottom out of three, and just the top out of the fourth. Tape them together with metal tape. Get some plastic go cups and a can of lighter fluid. Poke a small hole in the bottom can. Squirt just a small amount of lighter fluid into the tube, place the plastic go cup on top, and hold a cigarette lighter to the small hole. Damn if it doesn't sound close to the real thing. In our case, when we fired the first time, a nervous Thai security guard showed up. It was okay after we taught him how it worked.

(139) Did you bring home any souvenirs?

Danang: Piece of scrap metal, most of a .45-Cal pistol, a Seiko watch, a Hong Kong ordered suit, and a Sony tape recorder.

Udorn /Korat: N/A.

(140) Did you have a camera while with the 366?

Danang, Udorn, Korat: Yes, I had a camera and have a group of pictures.

(141) Did you keep a diary or notes of events? I did not keep a diary or any notes, but I did take a lot of pictures.

Danang, Udorn, and Korat: Still have some tapes, and my wife kept some letters.

(142) Do you have names and addresses of any of your buddies not on our roster?

Danang, Udorn, and Korat: I found some names on the orders while reviewing papers for the questions; however, I do not have addresses and have lost contact with most. Only one was contacted after retirement.

(143) Have any of your buddies passed away who have not been listed in the called-to-high-command registry? Please advise so they can join with their comrades in the listing on the memorial pages.

Chapter 4
Questions 201–233

(201) What aircraft did your unit use?

Danang: Upon arrival, I was strictly assigned to the squadron aircraft, F/4C. Later when I was reassigned to a Field Maintenance Squadron (FMS), I worked on all aircraft which included: C-123/Ranch Hands, PBY/Flying boats, C-130, C-121, A-1E, commercial aircraft, helicopters, and anything that could fly.

F/4 Phantom

Udorn: HH-53 C & Ds strictly. On this tour I worked strictly for the squadron, Fortieth ARRS.

Brand new HH-53D off an aircraft carrier.

Korat/Bien Hoa RVN: A-7D and only A-7Ds.

A-7D Quick Turn Around, Bien Hoa RVN 1972.

(202) What were their good points?

Danang: The F4 was an easy aircraft to maintain from both hydraulic and pneumatic standpoints—three hydraulic systems and one pneumatic system.

Udorn: The HH53, a modified navy helicopter, was a total surprise. Normally when you think of a helicopter you do not think *complicated*, and based on what little past helicopter experience I had, the 53 was a surprise. It has four hydraulic systems, one of which operates at 4500 PSI. Most components are easy to gain access to. The 53 could and did take a licking and keep on ticking.

Korat: The A7D is another modified navy bird and also had three hydraulic systems. It did not require much maintenance, and turn-around was faster than the F4.

(203) What didn't you like about them?

Danang: The main problem with maintaining the hydraulic system in the F4 is gaining access to the components. It takes many screw and panel removals to get at some of the major components.

Udorn: I cannot think of anything I disliked about the HH53s.

Korat: It had a similar problem concerning access to components as the F4, however not as bad.

(204) What was your unit's aircraft I.D. (number, tail code, painted markings)? i.e. A6, a, c, l, mo, color bands, stripes, etc.

Danang: The F-4C&Ds were known as the Phantom II, and later the F4s belonging to the 366th became known as "Gunfighters."

Udorn: HH-53C&D, Super Jolly Green Giant.

Korat: A-7D, Sometimes "Sandy" and sometimes just "D."

(205) Your aircraft's I.D.? (i.e. B52-H, FU-914, LC234.)

All: Same as 204.

(206) What nose art/personalized name did your aircraft use? Who painted it? Do you have a photo of it?

None of the aircraft had any special markings. The A-7Ds I left at England AFB had the sign of the flying Tiger, "Tiger Teeth." The aircraft on this TDY only had the squadron emblem.

(207) Number of flying hours? N/A.

I was not on flying status, and all of my flying was strictly as maintenance support. I did get the hydraulic specialist on flying status that replaced me at Udorn. The importance of flying status meant you received more pay. Also extra pay was earned when you went into a combat zone—"combat pay."

(208) Number of 366 combat hours? N/A.

(209) Wingman? N/A.

(210) Type of missions flown? N/A.

(211) What type gave you concern? N/A. Type you liked best? N/A.

(212) What was the greatest risks in strafing attacks? N/A.

   Dive bombing? N/A.

(213) Your assessment of enemy pilots and their aircraft that you encountered: N/A.

(214) What was the best point to hit the enemy's aircraft for a Kill (by type)? N/A.

(215)? N/A.

(216) What was your aircraft's most vulnerable point? N/A.

(217) Have you evaded SAM's? (Surface-to-air missiles are rockets fired at our aircraft in North Vietnam): N/A. *What countermeasures were employed?*

N/A.

(218) Were you ever shot down? N/A. *Over enemy area?* N/A.

   What was hit? N/A.

(219) Cause: air-to-air combat with (type of aircraft)? N/A.

(220) Did you bail out? N/A.

(221) Did you evade capture? N/A.

(222) If captured, by who? N/A.

(223) What POW prison were you at? N/A.

(224) Were you part of an escape? N/A.

(225) How were you treated? N/A.

(226) What was the most damage your aircraft sustained and still made it back? N/A.

(227) What was your most hazardous mission?

>   *Most interesting?*

>   *Most memorable?*

>   *Most enjoyable?*

(228) Were you ever assigned to temporary forward air/ground control duty? Describe: N/A

(229) Do you have a flight log we can copy? N/A.

(230) Do you have any gun camera film we can borrow? N/A.

(231) What flight did you fly in? N/A.

(232) Did you assume any other duties beside pilot or WSO? N/A.

(233) What auxiliary aircraft (HACK) did the unit have?

Danang: The base had just about any kind of aircraft: Ranch Hands, Flying boats (PBY's), C-130, C-121, A-1E, commercial aircraft, helicopters, and anything else that flew to include army, navy, and marine aircraft.

Udorn: HH53 C & Ds strictly. On this tour I worked strictly for the squadron.

Korat: A-D and only A7Ds.

Chapter 5
Questions 302–328

(302) What were your aircraft's I.D. number/letters?

Danang: F-4Cs or the Phantom IIs, and the aircraft that belonged to the 366th Fighter Squadron were known as "Gunfighters."

Udorn: HH-53C&D, The Super Jolly Green Giant, Big Ugly Fat Fellow, "BUFFs," or Super Jolly.

Korat: A-7D, Sometimes Sandy, or Big "D."

(303) Who was in your crew and what was their assignment?

Danang, Udorn, Korat: N/A.

(304) Was the crew assigned to a given aircraft? Revetments? More than one? Rotated within the flight?

Danang: Only the crew chief was assigned to one aircraft. The aircraft were assigned specific revetments. If I remember correctly, names were stenciled on the side of the aircraft, but that did not necessarily indicate they were the only one to fly that particular F4.

Udorn, Korat: Again, only the crew chiefs were assigned a particular aircraft. None of the aircraft had names stenciled on them.

(305) Name the pilots that were assigned to your aircraft date/ replaced.

The question keyed an incident that happened on the Udorn trip. It appeared as a small side note in The *Pacific Stars and Stripes*, Vol. 26, No. 30, Saturday, January 31, 1970: *MIG downs helo—US jets duel guns in North.*

Nearly two hours later, the Pentagon said an air force search and rescue helicopter looking for survivors was attacked and shot down by a Russian-built MIG21 fighter "in the vicinity of the North Vietnam-Laotian border." "US aircraft have been lost over North Vietnam in such operations since the bombing halt," officials said, but this was the first time they could recall a rescue helicopter being downed by an MIG.

Facts: It was definitely in Laos, and it involved two Jollys. The reason they knew it was a MIG21 was that the other Jolly saw it. The other crew saw the missile go up the Jolly's ramp and blow up. The aft ramp was always halfway down when on the other side of the fence, mainly because that was where one of the mini guns was mounted. One of the crewmembers was named Capt. Holly G. Bell; one enlisted (Flight Engineer Marvin E. Bell) was killed in a different incident. They were not related. For some unknown reason, their names stick—maybe because I remember getting drunk and buying a large brass bell, which I still have.

http://www.nexus.net: "Tail No: 66-14434 Model: HH-53B Date of Loss: 28 January 1970
Unit: Fortieth ARRS Country of Loss: NVN Call Sign: Jolly Green 71
Pilot: Holly G. Bell (14W-73)
Copilot: Leonard C. Leeser (14W-75)
Flight Engineer: William C. Shinn (14W-77)
PJ: William D. Pruett (14W-76)
PJ: William C. Sutton (14W-77)
Other: Gregory L. Anderson (photographer) (14W-73)
Notes: hit by missile fired from MIG during SAR for Seabird 02 (F-105G). The Mig-21 was piloted by Vu Ngoc Dinh who then had six total kills. He was with the 921st Flight Regiment.

Tail No: 68-8283 Model: HH-53C Date of Loss: 30 June 1970 Unit Fortieth ARRS
Country of Loss: Laos Call Sign: Jolly Green 54
Pilot: Leroy C. Schaneberg (09W-17)
Copilot: John W. Goeglein (09W-104)
Flight Engineer: Marvin E. Bell (09W-102)
PJ Paul L. Jenkins (09W-102)
PJ Michael F. Dean (09W-103)"

The above (14W-75) numbers and letters indicate where the name can be found on the Vietnam Memorial Wall in Washington DC. I have not had the opportunity to see the wall but I did get to see the portable wall that traveled around the States. What you see when you stand in front of it, is your reflection staring back.

Notes: "Hit by ground fire during SAR for NAIL 44 (OV-10A), crash site excavated DEA 93, remains identified as a group 7 March 1995."
Additional Notes: From John Waresh, A-1 Pilot (Ed: John Waresh remembers this as a Knife [Twenty-First SOS] helicopter that was shot down. It was actually a Fortieth ARRS HH-53C that was lost with all hands):

"Hi Jim: I was there in '70 and no, there are no pictures that I know of.

"So, you were a Knife. I worked with you guys from time to time, but not a whole lot as I remember. One of the saddest days of my tour was seeing one of your birds do a loop and slamming into the turf upright but descending at a hellish rate. She blew into a huge ball of flame. I was told eight guys were on board. The Knives lived right behind our hooch (602nd) and I knew some of them but not all.

"I was Sandy 4 watching the SAR progress with an army FAC as on-scene commander. We protested, but Buffalo Chip, or whoever ran the show, insisted he remain on-scene commander because he was first on site. When he called in the Knife for a pickup, we again protested but were told to shut up. Right after he went into a hover over the survivor (a Heavy Hook SOG guy riding in the back of an OV-10), he took a big hit on the right side. I saw the huge flash and it wasn't small arms. He pulled off in a left climbing spiral. After completing a 360 climbing turn she pitched up and did a complete loop, descending at an ever-increasing rate. She hit upright but going down like a freight train. She blew sky high, no chance for any survivors.

"After that, the powers that be ordered the Sandys to take over and we prepped the area, brought in the number two Knives, picked up the survivor and RTB to NKP.

"Not a nice memory. John."

(306) How many times was your aircraft replaced? Why?

Danang: Unknown number of replacements. The reason was losses over North Vietnam, and the most obvious reason was rocket attacks.

Udorn: Losses caused the need for replacements. During my tour we would go to South Thailand and reassemble them either on the carriers or on the dock (photos). The new Jollys came wrapped in a white rubberlike sealant, to keep the salt water out. They sure looked strange. They had no blades, and that was the major part of the reassemble.

A brand new HH53 still in Christmas wrapping being lowered from a carrier.

Korat: I don't remember any losses.

(307) How many times did your aircraft receive major battle damage? What was damaged? Was damage repaired by your unit or the service unit?

Danang: Most battle-damaged aircraft were repaired locally, however a couple of times the aircraft was cannibalized heavily (cannibalization means it was used for parts to keep the other aircraft flying) and the remains were crated/boxed, and returned to the States. At the end of the tour I went to Nakon Phona to help repair an F/4 that landed and sheared off the nose gear.

Udorn: All repairs were made by us, and during my tour none were returned to the States. Of the trips into Laos and Cambodia to field recover aircraft, once was to the Plain of Jars (I think), once to a rice paddy in South Laos, and once to a place called "LS 98."

LS 98 Laos

Korat: Only minor battle damage, which was repaired locally. I did get to go back to Udorn to replace a hydraulic pump on one of our A/7s.

(308) How many times did it get major overhaul work? What about normal wear and tear?

All 3: All aircraft had items or components that required time changing. After so many hours of operation these components were changed. The old parts were returned to the States for overhaul, testing, and returned to the supply chain.

(309) How many times was it sent to the service unit? For what type of problem?

All 3: We were the service unit, except for major battle damage, and then the remains were crated and returned to the States.

(310) What major components were replaced during its time with your unit? Indicate cause: A = accident; B = battle damage; F = mechanical failure; W = normal wear.

All 3: All maintenance was accomplished using either a squadron specialist or specialists from a field maintenance squadron. This included:

83

time changes, scheduled maintenance, battle damage, mechanical failure, calibration, systems testing, parts changing, and tech order updates and anything else to make it work.

(311) What was the most unusual repair your crew made?

Danang: A trip to Nakhon Phanom Thailand to replace a nose strut that was damaged when the F-4 made an emergency landing on this PSP runway. (PSP is perforated steel plating used to make temporary runways; it is not the best thing for jet aircraft because if there are rocks or whatever on the runway the jet engine will suck them up and possibly get damaged.) The nose gear collapsed upon landing. We went in and made the necessary repairs and launched it back to Danang. This was a friendly base, of course. In Thailand, the city was not off limits. The barracks were one story and made of teak wood. I said to myself that if I had to return for a second tour, I would want to come to Thailand. Little did I know then.

Udorn: (1) Relocate to Nakhon Phanom, do magic, and keep them flying for a hot rescue. Most memorable contribution, which saved a life. (2) Plain of Jars to recover a downed Jolly. The condition was to get it out by dark or destroy it. (3) Rice paddy somewhere on the other side of the fence. (The fence means the border between Thailand and Laos or Thailand and Cambodia.) (4) Relocate to 98, the other side of fence.

Korat: I did make one trip back to Udorn to replace a hydraulic pump on an A7. Also, back into Bien Hoa, Vietnam (RVN) to support the A-7s in a quick turn operation. A quick turn operation was when the aircraft from Thailand would land and be reloaded and refueled and sent on another mission. Because the A7 had low maintenance problems, it was well-suited for that type of operation. Both the HH53 and the A/7 had a manufacturer's saying: "Aircraft flight time is only limited by the duration of the crew." Also, I survived another few rocket attacks. One night, we played a cruel joke on one of the new troops. We drew a bull's-eye in the middle of the barracks floor. The target included words about an unnatural act with/against Ho-Chi-Minh, and daring him to hit the target. That young man slept in a flak jacket and helmet. That's something we should not have done. Regardless, the target was not hit—as close does not count.

(312) What field modifications were made? Why?

Danang: I do not remember if it was a field modification or simply a different use of the system. The F-4s made better use of the external mounted 20mm cannon and became known as "Gun Fighters." (see #314).

Udorn: The CH-53 was originally a troop carrier for the navy/marines. It was modified for Air Rescue for the air force. Part of the modification was the addition of three small 7.62mm, miniguns/Gatling guns, which gave it a sting. Also added was a feature for in-flight refueling. One of the Jollys was later modified for night recovery testing. We called this one the Green *Ka-Toy*. Don't ask me why. Ka-toy means queer in Thai. The "C" Cargo was changed from Cargo to "H" for rescue, thus HH-53.

Korat: Keep in mind the A-7D was originally a navy bird that was modified by the manufacturer to meet air force needs.

(313) Describe your pre-flight procedure for each type crewed.

All 3: The crew chief did his checklist and the crew followed theirs.

(314) How long did it take to modify the early F-4s to carry gun pods? What was involved? What was the maximum number carried? Were all the unit's F-4s modified? Or were replacements made?

Time? (Photos?)

Danang: (see #312) From: *Gunfighter Gazette.* Volume I, No. I, DaNang Air Base, Vietnam, June 29, 1967: Gunfighter—1967 Vintage.

> In this age of sophisticated jet aircraft and weaponry, the term *gunfighter* brings to mind something of the old west, where the man wearing an often used, low slung Colt .44 was someone to be reckoned with. The men of the 366th Tactical Fighter Wing here have dusted off the term and have applied it to their own MIG hunting missions. Now officially recognized as the Gunfighters, DaNang pilots earned the distinction by downing four

MIGs in aerial combat utilizing the pod-mounted 20mm Vulcan Gatling gun, slung under the bellies of their sleek F-4C Phantom IIs. It was not easy to earn the Gunfighter trademark. Conceived by Col. Frederick C. Blesse, 366th deputy commander for operations, it took some time before the idea could be battle tested. Colonel Blesse's idea was to carry the gun pod on MIG combat air patrols while flying escort missions for F-105 Thunderchiefs. He felt the gun pods would furnish added firepower where it was most needed—for the close aerial fighting inside the normal air-to-air missile range. Many problems had to be ironed out before the first *go;* would the pod reduce the aircraft's maneuverability in a dogfight? Would it cause fuel problems? What kind of site would be best? Along with the many problems, the assistance of literally hundreds of base personnel was required to make the idea work. Members of the Munitions Maintenance Squadron went into high gear. The gun had to function in a completely reliable manner for MIG CAP missions. Munitions personnel gave each gun going north that extra special care that could mean the difference in a tight spot. Munitions loading teams toiled, putting in overtime hours to assure that the gun, as well as other gunfighter ordnance, was properly hung and ready for the missions in the skies over Hanoi. F-4C Phantom II crew chiefs added the gun to their already-long checklists of items to inspect and okay before and after each flight. Tactical planners wrung the idea dry, looking for flaws and methods of improvement. Pilots too, had their skull sessions about the gun: aerial engagement tactics, arming techniques, talks from the munitions maintenance and weapons experts on how best to use the weapon, length of bursts, etc. One by one, the problems were nailed down and answered. Approval for use of the innovation was granted by Headquarters, Seventh Air Force, and the guns were mounted on several MIG CAP Phantoms for the acid test. Results were not long in coming—for in one afternoon in the skies near Hanoi, the whole complex scheme justified itself with the downing of two MIGs in almost as many minutes on May 14. Two Phantom Gunfighter crews, Maj. James A. Hargrove Jr., aircraft commander; 1st Lt. Stephen F. Demuth, pilot; Capt. James T. Craig Jr., aircraft commander; and 1st Lt. James T.Tally, pilot, were the first to lay claim to the Gunfighter title, both for themselves and the 366th Wing. It happened, in a few tense seconds, this way: Major Hargrove said, "We saw two MIGs below us, following two F-105s. I rolled in on them and fired at the lead ship with a missile, and missed. I reversed and again tried but missed with another missile. "By this time, the MIG was well inside our missile range, and I selected the gun. I began firing at around two thousand feet with a very rapid rate of closure. I lead him quite a bit, and the train of fire drifted down into him." Jubilant and enthusiastic pilots landed at DaNang that evening, full of confidence that the gun was just what was needed for the close infighting. Then a proven fact, all CAP flights from DaNang going into the Hanoi area on escort missions had several of their members equipped with the gun. It had accounted for two more MIG kills. On May 22, Lt. Col. Robert F. Titus, commander of the 389th TFS and his pilot, 1st Lt. Milan Zimer, blasted a MIG from the skies using the gun, and also became triple MIG killers on that mission. The most recent Gunfighter-style MIG killers are Maj. Durward K. Priester and Capt. John E. Pankhurst. Showing exceptional marksmanship with the use of his Gatling gun, Major Priester fired only 203 rounds of 20mm ammunition in downing the MIG. Some pilots call it the gun—others refer to it as the pistol, but any way it is described, the description is one of glowing and satisfied terms. Some say it looks odd slung on the centerline pylon of the Phantom II, graceless and clumsy. But to the pilot and ground crew, it is a symbol of success and status for the 366th Tactical Fighter Wing Gunfighters.

END This weekly newsletter was previously known as the *Danang Hilights.*

Jim Downey

(315) What different ordnance loads were used? Was napalm used? When was each type first used by your unit?

Danang: If you can dream of the load, the F-4 carried it (photos).

Udorn: The HH53 had three Miniguns, 7.62mm Gatling guns, and that was the only weapon loaded, except for a wide variation of personal arms carried by the crews. Talk about something to operate, on one of the trips across the fence, I test fired one, squeeze trigger on the right for two thousand rounds a minute. Then when you find the target with the tracers, you squeeze the trigger on the left for six thousand rounds a minute and the target disappears.

Korat: Any kind of load plus the A-7 had a built-in Gatling gun, 20mm cannon. On "Sandy" missions, gas was used. Gas made the bad guys sick—and the good guys sick, too, if they didn't have protection. With everyone on the ground sick, the PJs had no problem picking up the sick good guys and carrying them back to the penetrator for the trip back up the hoist to the chopper. A penetrator is the heavy combination jungle penetrator and chair type equipment capable of—in a sense—seating two people for the ride back up to the chopper. I'm not sure if the A7 carried the gas, but the old A1Es did.

(316) How long did it take to "rearm" your aircraft? What was your fastest time?

The only time quick rearm was important was when we relocated back to Bien Hoa to quick turn the A7. You can quick turn an A7, bomb, bullets, oil, and gas in minutes, faster with hot refueling. Hot refueling is when the aircraft is left running at a refueling pit somewhere between the end of the runway and the ramp or revetments area.

(317) Did you modify or build any equipment to help with the rearming?

Not with rearming.

(318) What was the most common problem with the radios? With the instruments?

Unknown.

(319) What was the frequency of repair for the avionics? What about for the weapons system units?

Unknown.

(320) How long did it take to refuel your aircraft, both on the ground and aerially?

If I remember correctly, the F4 was the first to use hot refueling, meaning that the engines were still running, and it was done prior to returning to the parking ramp. All three aircraft were capable of inflight refueling. Inflight refueling a helicopter was the most risky—think about it. The chopper flies as fast as possible with a large, hollow pole stuck out the front of it and tries to spear a big badminton birdie on the end of a hose hanging out of an airplane in the lead. All this goes on while the helicopter blades go round and round within feet of the hose. It's something like making love in space, with your hands and feet tied underneath and very close to a ceiling fan operating at full speed.

(321) What was the most difficult part of the crew's job?

Unknown, assuming you are talking about the flight crew. If you are talking about us maintenance weenies, the hardest part was working in the heat. Sometimes the surface of the aircraft was so hot that we had to carry bundles of rags, so we could kneel on the top surfaces without burning ourselves. Hot, damn hot. We did get a fine tan. On the Jolly tour I got so dark that some of the natives thought I was Mexican, until I showed the part of me that the sun does not shine on. I might add that this is what probably contributed to the skin cancer that I am currently receiving treatment for every six months.

Jim Downey

(322) What was your flight line area like? Did you use a hangar?

Danang: At first we used the old French revetments, two or three F-4 per revetment. No hangar. Later on, for major maintenance jobs, we used a large hangar at the other end of the flight line, as that was soon to be the location of the field maintenance unit.

Udorn: Metal revetments filled with sand. We did have one covered hangar for major maintenance.

Korat: It was an open ramp, with hangar space if needed. At Ben Hoa there were concrete revetments. A few had holes because of rocket hits.

A hardened revetment that was hit by a rocket.

(323) Were your revetments open? Sheltered from the weather? Protected from strafing, mortar or rocket attack? Other?

F4 aircraft in revetment at Danang RVN.

Danang: Open revetments for aircraft. When I returned for the second time, the French revetments had been replaced with hard-covered revetments for some protection against rockets. Personnel had access to bunkers made of sandbags, and on the flight line sandbags above the ground equaled a foxhole.

Udorn: Open revetments and during my tour no rocket attacks.

Korat: Open parking area. On the trip back to Bien Hoa, the A7's were parked under concrete-covered revetments. Some had holes in the top from receiving direct hits.

(324) Did they have permanent hardstands? Metal plated? (If so, what type?) Was there any shelter for the crew such as tents or shacks?

Danang, Udorn, Korat: Blacktop or concrete was the norm with line shacks or conex boxes.

(325) Were there any improvements made while at the base?

Danang: Many improvements. From dirt floor tents to two-story barracks, from four-holer outhouse to real flush-em-ups, from field kitchen to dining hall.

Udorn: None noticeable.

Korat: No improvements were needed as the compound used was the officers' section of an empty army compound. Everything was available, including a swimming pool.

(326) What tools and equipment did you have? Where were they stored? Did you use any captured equipment? What type? How was it obtained?

Danang: Standard issue tool box. Shop was a cardboard Quonset hut (photo). When not in use they were left in the shop.

Maintenance shack at Danang RVN 1966.

Udorn: A small building shared with other specialists (photos).

Korat: Large shop/building shared with other aircraft specialists.

(327) How far was your line area from the living area?* How did you get back and forth?* (walk, bicycle, motorcycle, line vehicle, bus?)

Danang: At first you strictly walked. Later there was a bus route, nothing spectacular. We did have step-vans on the ramp.

Udorn: Bus.

Korat: Bus.

(328) Did you use a vehicle as part of your job? What type? For what? Did it have a personalized name? Was it "G.I."?

Danang: The bus was the major form of transportation, or walking. There was a flatbed trailer used to transport troops back and forth to China Beach (photo).

Udorn: Squadron had pickup trucks. Otherwise there was a scheduled bus route.

Korat: Toyota pickup trucks for the flight line and a scheduled bus route.

Chapter 6
Questions 401-422

(401) Describe your "non-flight line" area, i.e. AF tech supply, communications, fuel dump, intelligence, medical unit, mess hall, orderly room, operations, supply, photo lab, etc. Include photos if possible.

Danang: (Photos) As camp Danang grew from dirt floor tents and four-holer outhouses to having dining facilities, air conditioning, an NCO club, and air conditioned pilot quarters, it became easier and easier to live, which was great. Toward the end of 1967, a hospital unit was located in Camp Danang—shortly to be called Gunfighter Village. The main cantonment area contained the NCO club, officers' club, twenty-four-hour mess hall, and a theater.

Udorn: This was a pretty good-sized base and even included friends of Air America/Central Intelligence Agency (CIA). The work area or flight line area was on the opposite side of the runway from the barracks area, thus not readily within walking distance.

Korat: (Photos) The sleeping area was in an old army base adjacent to the air base. A bus was the normal mode of transportation. The TDY to Bien Hoa RVN was to another reduced-staff base, and the barracks were within walking distance. By reduced staff, I mean that Vietnam was slowly being reduced in the number of American military personnel left in country.

(402) Describe the work you performed.

I was a hydraulic specialist, responsible for repairing, maintaining, and troubleshooting aircraft hydraulic and pneumatic systems. I was good, and really enjoyed it. On the second trip with the Jollys it got to the point where I could nearly take the pulse of the chopper's hydraulic system and tell you what was wrong. You could do something with your hands and mind and see it work, no smoke and no mirrors, plus the paperwork part was minor. You could make repairs and feel comfortable enough to bet your life on it/fly on it. When I first arrived at the rescue squadron, I was taken to the flight line (still in class A uniform), because they did not have a hydraulic specialist and they were having flight controls troubles. Keep in mind that I had not attended a technical school on the HH-53 because there was none.

Also I had the impression that this was going to be a cushy job. After all, how complicated could a helicopter hydraulic system be? Talk about a mind overload; this bird had four hydraulic systems, while most aircraft only had three. One of the systems operated at 4,500 psi (pounds per square inch). The problem with the flight controls dealt with the tail rotor servo/cylinder. Seems that they had replaced it three or more times and it still would not check out. Everything had been done by the book, but it still would not check out. After about an hour I figured it out: the adjustments to cylinder length. The technical manual only addressed fine adjustments and forgot to include large adjustments. After we made those adjustments, everything checked out. Needless to say, they loved me. Later, one of the Jollys developed an APU problem. The auxiliary power unit (APU) is really a small jet engine that provided hydraulic and electrical power until the engines are started. The APU is started hydraulically with an accumulator. The accumulator charge is only good for one try to start the APU. If the APU doesn't start, then the accumulator must be recharged by hand by pumping the accumulator to 3,000 psi (pounds per square inch). This took many, many, many strokes of the hand pump. Plus, when the APU did not start everyone could hear it. It sounded like a high-pitched whine that plays out. Needless to say, laughter would break out in the squadron maintenance area because everyone could hear it, and knew someone was going to have to pump the system back up. After I learned of the problem, I borrowed a hydraulic mule from the F-4 unit at Udorn. A hydraulic mule is an external engine-driven unit that provides hydraulic pressure to aircraft so the engine or engines do not have to be run to check out the systems. We hooked the mule up after making a set of adapter couplings so both the mule and the aircraft hydraulic system could work at the same time. We then tried to start the APU, and it failed, and while everyone was seeing whose APU did not start they were getting ready to laugh and point. We fired it off again, and about fifteen seconds later, fired it off a third time. Needless to say, people were coming from the other revetments and the squadron maintenance buildings and offices. They wanted to see this big dude who could pump that accumulator up so fast. They really fell in love with me then. Keep in mind that the HH-53s were so new to the air force that there were no technical schools. I found out that the marines at Danang had the same type of aircraft, and I asked to go and talk with their technical represents (civilian specialists from the manufacture, Sikorsky). I spent two or three days with these guys and picked up all kinds of good stuff. They were located back at Danang on the coast south of China Beach. That is how I returned to Danang and discovered all the changes. The tech reps I talked to told me that they had made a mistake, and I went into the field to help them recover a downed marine chopper. The dudes he went with broke the one they went in on so they could stay the night. By *broke* I mean that maintenance troops can make decisions about whether a plane is safe to fly or not. In this case they probably made that call for some small problem that would remedy itself the next morning. Typical marines, they were on top of a mountain and would holler nasty comments about whether or not Ho Chi Minh knew who his daddy was. He said that was the last time he went anywhere with them.

(403) Which base had the best setup for your work?

They all had about the same setup, except when I first arrived at Danang there were no shop test stands or other test equipment until I moved in with the field maintenance shop. Udorn did not have fancy test equipment, so I designed and built a piece of test equipment that did everything we needed (see #134). If it was something special I needed, I could go to the F-4s hydraulic shop. On one of the paddy recoveries, we kept having flight control troubles. The pilot had ordered the crew to bail out, thinking he was going to lose control. The two PJs and the copilot injured themselves bailing out and the flight engineer refused to jump. They were both fixing to jump when the jungle opened up and they were able to put it down in a rice paddy. The chopper would automatically switch back and forth to the backup hydraulic system, causing the chopper to jump. After we got it home to Udorn, I tried everything I knew to find it on the ground—but no success. The squadron did not have an instrument technician, so we asked to borrow one from the F-4 Squadron Field Maintenance unit. The young man they sent had elongated pupils, something like cat's eyes only going the other direction. Because we could not find it on the ground, we asked for some inflight testing. Talk about making a pilot happy—just tell one to do his stuff at low altitude to try to make the bird change systems. He would first stand the chopper on its nose, then its tail, and then a tight turn. We all swore up and down that we had caused the instrument troop eyes to be round, or at least appear to be round. Keep in mind we were standing up walking around trying to find the problem, and also remember that you can spin a bucket of water over your head, and you won't lose a drop if you do not stop on the top of the spin. Disney would call it an "E" ticket ride. We eventually found a loose wire on a terminal strip that would drop ground when it felt like it. (Dropping the electrical ground is like a switch, and the electrical circuit is no longer complete.) Also, I remember one time one of the choppers returned with an unsafe landing gear indication. So I was sent to the infield (grassy area near the runways) with the landing gear safety pins. All I had to do when the chopper hovered above me was reach up and install the pins. A helicopter generates a lot of static electricity, and needless to say I was knocked on my ass. I found out later I was supposed to wait until the rescue hook was touching the ground, so the static electricity would be discharged. Maybe it was my initiation?

Korat: Had a full-fledged shop with all the necessary test equipment.

(404) List the type of equipment your work area had: i.e. adding machine; air conditioner; computer; copy machine; electronic test gear; lathe; mimeograph; movie projector; power generator; radio (two-way); telephone; typewriter, etc.

Danang: The first shop at Danang was a cardboard Quonset hut. Later when the specialists were combined into the Field Maintenance Squadron, I moved into a large hanger. We acquired a hydraulic test stand, and later air conditioning. Talk about progress.

Udorn: We shared a small shop with other specialists—only desks and work benches.

Korat: A full-fledged shop, test stand, bench stock, air conditioning, and separate transportation to and from the aircraft.

(405) Did you use a vehicle in your job? What type? How was it used? Did it have a personalized name? Was it "G.I." issued? Captive?

Normally transportation was provided to and from the flight line, because of the tool boxes, replacement parts, and any troubleshooting gear that was needed. Also, sometimes we had to return to the shops for small bench stock items such as seals.

(406) What events do you remember the best involving your job?

Danang: Going after the downed F4 in Thailand. (See question #311.)

Udorn: Going into the field to recover down choppers, and being successful. (See questions 133 and 135.)

Korat: Relocation, TDY to BIEN HOA for quick reloads/turnaround of the A7D.

(407) What type of equipment did the weather Det. have? Where was it located?

Unknown.

(408) What type of equipment did the control tower have? Mobile? Fixed?

Unknown.

(409) What equipment did the crash crew have? What unit was it assigned to?

Danang: When your term "crash crew" was mentioned I immediately remember the time at Danang when a heavy rocket attack damaged a bunch of F-4s on the flight line and they were burning. One was upside down on top of one of the revetments (see #322). The revetments at this time were left over by the French and consisted of sand and cement about twelve feet high and two or three feet wide. Corrugated metal frames were also starting to be used. They too were about twelve feet high and three to four feet wide filled with sand (photos). A crash crew rolled up (two trucks) and was attempting to put out the fire when the plane blew, killing all of the crash crew. The only things left were two burned out fire trucks. I had taken pictures, but they never made it back from the developer. Follow up: "July 15, 1967, twenty minutes after midnight, Charlie launched eighty-three rockets at the air strip. Ten aircraft were totally destroyed, forty-nine damaged, 174 wounded and nine killed." (http://www.virtualwall.orgdbBrooksJF01a.htm)

(410) Do you remember the number of the engineering BN (AVN) that was responsible for building and repair of runways?

Unknown, but most likely the navy Seabees.

(411) How close was the nearest defense position to your work area? Living area? Was it against air or ground attack? What armament? (for example, Quad. 50s 40mm)

Danang: Sand bag bunkers were everywhere. Also sand bags (above-ground foxholes) were around. Every now and then the covered bunkers would have to be rebuilt. On one occasion when an aircraft crashed, two covered bunkers collapsed. After that happened I always wondered if the covered bunkers were, in fact, a safe place to go. One thing to keep in mind is that we air force weenies carried no weapons at Danang. They were locked up for safety. When I landed at a remote field while taking an in-country R&R (rest and recuperation) and going to visit my cousin at ANKE (RVN), I was not allowed off the aircraft because I was not armed—another bad case of young and stupid.

Udorn: When we crossed the fence we were issued weapons. We did not need defensive positions, but the aircraft were in revetments just in case. I think Nakhon Phanom RTAFB had been rocketed once. So the northern part of Thailand was not necessarily secured. We did use a remote field in North Thailand that was called McNamara's Folly, because it was constructed to be a B52 Base, then it was discovered to be too close to the fence/border for the security of/for the B-52s that were scheduled to use it. When we crossed the fence, we left all identification behind to the extent that we did not even wear rank or name labels on our shirts.

A younger Jim.

Korat: No protection except for Thai guards. On the Bien Hoa TDY we played musical bunkers when necessary, and the aircraft were reloaded in covered revetments. The Vietnamese kept spare F-5s in covered revetments across from our area, maybe two hundred feet apart. The thing that came to your attention here was that some of these reinforced concrete revetments had holes in the tops because of rocket hits. Even in this condition, we did not have access to weapons. Talk about stupid. Keep in mind that this was 1972 and the reduction had started. That's why the officers' club and the NCO club were in the same building at Bien Hoa (RVN).

(412) Do you remember the number of the A Artillery unit that protected the 366?

No such thing.

(413) How close was the nearest personnel protection shelter against bombing, mortar rocket, and strafing attacks to your living area/work area? What was it—bomb shelter, bunker, trench, or other? How often was it used?

This was only a problem in Vietnam. While in the tents, the nearest sandbagged foxhole was just outside the tent. The reason that most foxholes were above ground was because of the rainy season. It wouldn't be too bad to dive into a hole of water—except for what creature or razor blade trap would be waiting on you. The barracks had covered sandbag bunkers next to each building. Rocket attacks were usually over in less than a minute and involved less than ten rockets. More dudes were hurt getting to cover. The smart bet was to simply hit the dirt. Of course if you were on a second floor, you needed to work your way down to the dirt. After we moved into the two-story barracks and after a rocket attack, you could usually count on finding some new dude knocked out because he had run into the 4x4s on the first floor that held up the second floor.

(414) Did you receive any defense combat training while with the 366?

On-the-job training.

(415) What weapon were you issued? Did you have any captured weapons?

Danang: US Air Force dudes were not issued weapons at Danang. Supposedly they were immediately available in a conex box somewhere in the compound.

Udorn: When we crossed the fence to recover a downed chopper we were issued everything, M-16, and bandolier of ammo, .38-cal revolver and ammo, survival vest, and extra radio. I brought back a Chinese Mosin Nagant rifle and a Russian SKS rifle legally on this trip. I had traded Polaroid film and a Seiko watch for them, compliments of the little dudes at 98/Laos. By *little dudes* I mean most of the fighters in Laos were children, and in a lot of cases the rifles they carried were taller than they were. That is another stupid part of war; little children were made into warriors with old faces. Once again fate was on my side—in the military school I attended the last two years of high school, I was too skinny for football and too smart to be a tackling dummy, so I was on the rifle team. Columbia Military Academy, Columbia, Tennessee. Class of 1958.

Udorn: Nothing.

(416) Was your area ever damaged by enemy action? Your equipment?

Danang: Rocket attacks randomly selected different parts of the flight line and base for targets. It was more like playing Russian roulette with rockets because most of the time valuable targets were missed. By money targets, I mean aircraft. Lives were lost, and to that individual, friends, and family, it was worth more than the money targets. Danang was known as Rocket City because of the frequent attacks.

(417) What were the duty schedule and living conditions like while stationed at Alexandria AFB (later England AFB), Louisiana or Holloman AFB, Mexico? Photos?

I was reassigned to England AFB in 1972 just prior to returning to Korat for the third trip. In 1978 I retired and stayed in Alexandria, Louisiana. In 1992 England Air Force Base Louisiana closed. It was the best-kept secret in the air force. My daughter Debbie's marriage was the last marriage performed on base. My other daughter (Jennifer) was also married on that base.

(418) What training and maneuvers were you involved with?

Vietnam was the primary training ground during my tour of duty. Early on, while in SAC (Strategic Air Command), alerts were called, and loaded aircraft were launched and prepared for war.

(419) Describe your cold war assignment for NATO in France/ Italy/other: N/A.

(420) What was the situation during the Cuban missile crisis?

I had just re-enlisted for the first time and was home in McKenzie, Tennessee, on leave. I received a telegram telling me to report back to McCoy AFB FLA. When I returned, all the B-52s had left and there were aircraft of all types everywhere on base. I was able to work on all kinds of aircraft, the most memorable being a KB-50. I had to go to the fire department to borrow a wrench big enough to tighten one of the hydraulic lines. The U2s had taken over our hangar, and that was very interesting. Naturally, we did not work on them because they had their own maintenance troops.

(421) What activities were you involved with while at Mt. Home AFB? Panama? Desert Storm?

I retired November 1, 1978. I did have a son-in-law who got to play the Desert Storm Game. Talk about doing it right; Desert Storm was how Vietnam should have been handled. If nothing else, maybe the stupidity of Vietnam did save lives in the desert experience. Plus, no one—and I mean no one—hassled those troops returning from Desert Storm. I remember someone saying that we had finally won two in a row. Korea was a tie, Vietnam was a loss, and Granada and Desert Storm were winners.

(422) What impact has the new composite air intervention wing concept of the 366 had on you?

N/A.

Chapter 7
Death

Note: This is a paper from a college course. The course was "Death and Dying," and after my three trips to Vietnam, I thought it appropriate.

October 2, 1991
"Death"

Death, where are you? The weak and the brave wonder about that question. Have you wondered too about that question? Have you tempted her? Of course you have, whether it was back when you were in the service or feeling your oats driving your car down the highway at a hundred miles per hour plus. What will she do to you? Put you in hell or let you look down upon others from a distant cloud? You say to yourself, *Am I afraid to die; will I be brave?* Yet you tempted her every chance you got. Maybe not the guy who tempts her by walking through the rice paddies of Vietnam—but the airplane mechanic who goes into places where the war is not supposed to be and climbs around on top of a sick helicopter, worth three million, in the wide open spaces of some country that is not supposed to be in the war, but really and truly is. A place called Laos. Here I am a target, wondering, *why?* Or maybe a troop in personnel who sits at a base in "Nam" with no weapon, taking numerous rocket attacks, and has friends killed because they flirted with death, and lost, or was it won? Takes the attacks because that is all he can do. He is not supposed to challenge the enemy just because he is the target or the cheese in the trap. Much later, my granddaughter reminded me: "The second mouse always gets the cheese." He must let someone else do the getting even with. Driving one hundred miles per hour down some dark road, will death catch me and make me have an accident? So what, at least I will not grow old and be put out to pasture, rejected by my children and life itself. All in the name of busy. Go ahead and tempt her. Death knows no age and welcomes all challengers. Who, me?

This is another short paper I wrote for another similar class.

September 14, 1983
"Death and the Self"

After skimming four books, I came to the conclusion that no one was going to give five or ten easy steps in dealing with death, or a, so to speak, "how to do it" book. All the books agree on one major point. Sooner or later everyone is going to die, or tactfully put: "All the academic degrees and professional certifications in the world do not guarantee that one will be able to contemplate death in an open, sensitive, and balanced manner." I would add the word *experience* to the above quoted statement. In the introduction, the author included a statement tucked in a paragraph's end: "The reader is urged to protect himself at all times, while not closing his mind, etc." This statement has more real meaning than most people realize. In order to understand how to deal with our death, the author would have us understand the following:

"1. I am an individual with a life of my own, a personal existence.
2.   I belong to a class of beings, one of whose attributes is mortality.
3.   Using the intellectual process of logical deduction, I arrive at the conclusion that my personal death is a certainty.
4.   There are many possible causes of my death, and these causes might operate in many different combinations, although I might evade or escape one particular cause. I cannot evade all causes.
5.   My death will occur in the future. By future, I mean a time to live that has not yet elapsed.
6.   But I do not know when in the future my death will occur. The event is certain; the timing is uncertain.
7.   Death is a final event. My life ceases. This means that I will never again experience, think, or act, at least as a human being on this earth.
8.   Accordingly death is the ultimate separation of me from the world."

The eight parts of the above "I Will Die" is based on death as final, which is more an attitude than fact. It is also based on one individual's theory, which is a conclusion based on his personal life expectations. In other books, authors express their opinion of what death is when in fact it is unknown, and a person who finds out what it is will not be able to tell us. Maybe in the process of trying to understand death we should ask ourselves, *Why are we?* To pose a similar, around-the-corner theory: maybe we are PAC-MAN in/on the big C.R.T.? It takes another quarter for us to try the next step/game. How are we to know what death is when we don't know what life is? Now that we have left the question of *what is death* unanswered, let's move on to facing the thought of death, death and the self, or maybe, facing the unknown? Philosopher Jacques Choron distinguished three types of death fear: (a) what comes after death, (b) event of dying, and (c) "ceasing to be." Thus, fear of dying often involves other fears, i.e. "prolonged suffering, weakness, dependency, and loss of control," plus others, such as: will we be made to pay for our sins? Will we die by fire, suffocation, drowning? Will we know of the impending death? Will we experience the moment of death? etc. The two major concerns of death involve: (1) fear, and (2) anxiety. Some argue they are the same. These are further divided into self and others. *Self* being one's own death and *others* being friends, etc. Believe it or not, "self" is what I am trying to concentrate on.

Freud's statement "theoretical position which emphasized the function of anxiety in survival and adaptation" is probably the closet statement to an easy "how to do it" outline/statement I could find. He recommends discovering the source and taking further action. Freud also stated his doubt that there is such a phenomenon as *normal fear of death.* Based on all the run-around and dazzling word play, I assume that there is no magic list of things to do to cope with your own death—mainly because there are too many variables. Thus, you must handle it on your own in your own way. The next few paragraphs are about how one individual dealt with the increased odds of death during three trips to Vietnam. Going to Vietnam posed no real threat, because the individual has moved around constantly during his lifetime. What got his attention was when four friends jumped into what was thought to be a safe area that took a direct rocket hit. Three were killed outright and the fourth "survived" with the loss of all but one limb. This was just the first of similar experiences that caused this individual to seek a way to cope and maintain some sort of sanity. Actions taken were the following, which is not complete. I remember the quote "urged to protect himself."

    a.   Yoga and/or self-medication.
    b.   Become a loner.
    c.   Accepting facts that someone is trying to kill him or it is a game of Russian roulette in which someone else controls the gun.
    d.   Pay more attention to the inner self.
    e.   Pay less attention to religious belief because he was surely not in control, or it would not be happening.
    f.   Block the mood.

Even with these actions after each trip, his nerves became more uptight. In conclusion, I might add that with time and love after ten years, things are nearly back to normal with the exception that death doesn't seem to bother him.

Jim Downey

References:

1. Kastenbaum, Robert, and Ruth Aisenberg, *The Psychology of Death.* Springer Publishing Co., Inc. New York, 1972.
2. Bender, Hagen. *Death & Dying, Opposing Viewpoints.* Green haven Press, Inc. Minnesota, 1980.
3. Watson, *The Romeo Error,* Anchor Press / Doubleday, New York. 1975.

Instructor's comments: "Interesting presentation. I would have liked to have had the opportunity of talking with this friend of yours." Note: Of course *I* am my friend. After reading this again while trying to organize it, I am glad the VA did get a chance to read it or I would probably be labeled with PTSD in with the other medical determinations!

Conclusion

So: This all started because of my curiosity as to where my father's and my trails crossed in our travels. Draw a line from California to the Philippines, to Shanghai from 1930 to 1933, him via boat. Now draw a line from California to Saigon, Vietnam and back from Danang, Vietnam, 1966 to 1967. Then another line from California to Bangkok, Udorn, Nakhon Phonon, Thailand, Danang, Vietnam, 1969 to 1970. Then a line from England AFB, Alexandria, Louisiana to California to the Philippines, to Thailand, to Vietnam, to Laos, to Kadena, Okinawa, 1972 to 1973—me by air, him by sea. This does not include our trip together to and from Germany in 1948 and crossing his track in Europe during World War II that included Germany, France, and Holland.

Chapter 8
Travel Orders USAF

Travel times extracted from vouchers: Starting with the 319th Field Maintenance Squadron. Strategic Air Command. Grand Forks Air Force Base, North Dakota. 58201. To: 6252 Tactical Fighter Wing Pacific Air Command Air Force, APO. San Francisco, 96337.

23 MARCH 66............ GRAND FORKS AFB ND / DEPARTED
25 MARCH 66............ MCKENZIE TENN / ARRIVED
29 MARCH 66............ MCKENZIE TENN / DEPARTED
30 MARCH 66............ ORLANDO FLA / ARRIVED
11 APRIL 66............... ORLANDO FLA / DEPARTED
11 APRIL 66............... MACDILL FLA / ARRIVED
24 MAY 66 .... MACDILL FLA / DEPARTED
24 MAY 66 .... ORLANDO FLA / ARRIVED
05 AUGUST 66............ ORLANDO FLA / DEPARTED
05 AUGUST 66............ CHARLESTON AFB SC / ARRIVED
06 AUGUST 66............ CHARLESTON AFB SC / DEPARTED
07 AUGUST 66............ TRAVIS AFB CAL / ARRIVED
08 AUGUST 66............ TRAVIS AFB CAL / DEPARTED
08 AUGUST 66............ SAN FRANCISCO INTERNATIONAL / ARRIVED
08 AUGUST 66............ SAN FRANCISCO INTERNATIONAL / DEPARTED
09 AUGUST 66............ HAWAII INTERNATIONAL / ARRIVED
09 AUGUST 66............ HAWAII INTERNATIONAL / DEPARTED
09 AUGUST 66............ GUAM INTERNATIONAL / ARRIVED
09 AUGUST 66............ GUAM INTERNATIONAL / DEPARTED
10 AUGUST 66............ SAIGON RVN / ARRIVED
14 AUGUST 66............ SAIGON / DEPARTED
15 AUGUST 66............ DANANG RVN / ARRIVED
08 JULY 67................. DANANG RVN / DEPARTED
08 JULY 67................. NAKHON PHANOM THAILAND / ARRIVED
11 JULY 67................. NAKHON PHANOM THAILAND / DEPARTED
11 JULY 67................. DANANG RVN / ARRIVED
13 AUGUST 67............ DANANG RVN / DEPARTED
13 AUGUST 67............ NORTON AFB CAL / ARRIVED
13 AUGUST 67............ NORTON AFB CAL / DEPARTED
13 AUGUST 67............ LOS ANGLES CAL / ARRIVED

13 AUGUST 67 .... LOS ANGLES CAL / DEPARTED
14 AUGUST 67 .... ORLANDO FLA / ARRIVED
24 AUGUST 67 .... ORLANDO FLA / DEPARTED
01 SEPT 67 .... LUBBOCK TX / ARRIVED
05 SEPT 67 .... LUBBOCK TX / DEPARTED
05 SEPT 67 .... REESE AFB TX / ARRIVED

FROM: 3500 FIELD MAINTENANCE SQUADRON AIR FORCE
TRAINING COMMAND (ATC) REESE AIR FORCE BASE, TEXAS
79401 TO: FORTIETH AEROSPACE RESCUE / RECOVERY
SQUADRON, MILITARY AIR TRANSPORTATION COMMAND
(MAC) APO SAN FRANCISCO CAL 96237.

02 JUNE 69 .... REESE AFB TX / DEPARTED
05 JUNE 69 .... MCKENZIE TN / ARRIVED
10 JUNE 69 .... MCKENZIE TN / DEPARTED
11 JUNE 69 .... ORLANDO FLA / ARRIVED
04 JULY 69 .... ORLANDO FLA / DEPARTED
04 JULY 69 .... DALLAS TX / ARRIVED
04 JULY 69 .... DALLAS TX / DEPARTED
04 JULY 69 .... SAN FRANCISCO CAL / ARRIVED
04 JULY 69 .... SAN FRANCISCO CAL / DEPARTED
04 JULY 69 .... TRAVIS AFB CAL / ARRIVED
06 JULY 69 .... TRAVIS AFB CAL / DEPARTED
06 JULY 69 .... HAWAII INT / ARRIVED
06 JULY 69 .... HAWAII INT / DEPARTED
07 JULY 69 .... CLARK AFB PHIL / ARRIVED
07 JULY 69 .... CLARK AFB PHIL / DEPARTED
07 JULY 69 .... DONMONG RTAFB / ARRIVED
07 JULY 69 .... DONMONG RTAFB / DEPARTED
07 JULY 69 .... BANGKOK THAILAND / ARRIVED
09 JULY 69 .... BANGKOK THAILAND / DEPARTED
09 JULY 69 .... DONMONG RTAFB / ARRIVED
09 JULY 69 .... DONMONG RTAFB / DEPARTED
09 JULY 69 .... UDORN RTAFB / ARRIVED
31 AUGUST 69 .... UDORN RTAFB / DEPARTED
31 AUGUST 69 .... TUY-HOA RVN / ARRIVED
31 AUGUST 69 .... TUY-HOA RVN / DEPARTED
31 AUGUST 69 .... TAN SON NHUT RVN / ARRIVED
01 SEPT 69 .... TAN SON NHUT RVN / DEPARTED
01 SEPT 69 .... DANANG RVN / ARRIVED

05 SEPT 69 .... DANANG RVN / DEPARTED
05 SEPT 69 .... TAN SON NHUT RVN / ARRIVED
05 SEPT 69 .... TAN SON NHUT RVN / DEPARTED
05 SEPT 69 .... UDORN RTAFB / ARRIVED
25 OCT 69 .... UDORN RTAFB / DEPARTED
25 OCT 69 .... AMERICAN EMBASSY LAOS / ARRIVED
25 OCT 69 .... AMERICAN EMBASSY LAOS / DEPARTED
25 OCT 69 .... UDORN RTAFB / ARRIVED
05 DEC 69 .... UDORN RTAFB / DEPARTED
05 DEC 69 .... NAKHON PHANOM RTAFB / ARRIVED
07 DEC 69 .... NAKHON PHANOM RTAFB / DEPARTED
07 DEC 69 .... UDORN RTAFB / ARRIVED
08 FEB 70 .... UDORN RTAFB / DEPARTED
08 FEB 70 .... UTAPAO RTAFB / ARRIVED
08 FEB 70 .... UTAPAO RTAFB / DEPARTED
08 FEB 70 .... SATTAHIP THAILAND / ARRIVED
16 FEB 70 .... SATTAHIP THAILAND / DEPARTED
17 FEB 70 .... UTAPAO RTAFB / ARRIVED
17 FEB 70 .... UTAPAO RTAFB / DEPARTED
17 FEB 70 .... UDORN RTAFB / ARRIVED
21 MAR 70 .... UDORN RTAFB / DEPARTED
21 MAR 70 .... NAKHON PHANOM RTAFB

THAILAND AND OUS AIRA
AMERICAN EMBASSY, APO 96352 / ARRIVED

23 MAR 70 .... / DEPARTED
23 MAR 70 .... UDORN RTAFB / ARRIVED
05 JULY 70 .... UDORN RTAFB / DEPARTED
05 JULY 70 .... DONMONG RTAFB / ARRIVED
05 JULY 70 .... DONMONG RTAFB / DEPARTED
05 JULY 70 .... BANGKOK THAILAND / ARRIVED
05 JULY 70 .... BANGKOK THAILAND / DEPARTED
06 JULY 70 .... DOMONG RTAFB / ARRIVED
06 JULY 70 .... DOMONG RTAFB / DEPARTED
06 JULY 70 .... TRAVIS AFB CAL / ARRIVED
06 JULY 70 .... TRAVIS AFB CAL / DEPARTED
07 JULY 70 .... ORLANDO FLA / ARRIVED
16 JULY 70 .... ORLANDO FAL / DEPARTED
17 JULY 70 .... MCKENZIE TN / ARRIVED
21 JULY 70 .... MCKENZIE TN / DEPARTED

21 JULY 70 .... DALLAS TX / ARRIVED
22 JULY 70 .... DALLAS TX / DEPARTED
22 JULY 70 .... LUBBOCK TX / ARRIVED
25 JULY 70 .... LUBBOCK TX / DEPARTED
25 JULY 70 .... TUCSON ARIZ / ARRIVED

AUGUST 1972 : IN COUNTRY REASSIGNMENT TO ENGLAND AFB LA. 4472ND SUPPORT SQUADRON TACTICAL AIR COMMAND (TAC) DAVIS MONTHAN AFB, ARIZONA 85707. JCS DIRECTED DEPLOYMENT PLAN ID 9950A FROM: ENGLAND AIR FORCE BASE LOUISIANA TO: MYRTLE BEACH AIR FORCE BASE SOUTH CAROLINA 354TH TFW

15 OCT 72 .... ENGLAND AFB LA / DEPARTED
15 OCT 72 .... LOS ANGLES CAL / ARRIVED
15 OCT 72 .... LOS ANGLES CAL / DEPARTED
15 OCT 72 .... HONOLULU HAW / ARRIVED
15 OCT 72 .... HONOLULU HAW / DEPARTED
16 OCT 72 .... CLARK AFB PHIL / ARRIVED
17 OCT 72 .... CLARK AFB PHIL / DEPARTED
17 OCT 72 .... UTAPAO RTAFB THAI / ARRIVED
17 OCT 72 .... UTAPAO RTAFB THAI / DEPARTED
17 OCT 72 .... KORAT RTAFB / ARRIVED
25 NOV 72 .... KORAT RTAFB / DEPARTED
25 NOV 72 .... BIEN HOA RVN / ARRIVED
10 DEC 72 .... BIEN HOA RVN / DEPARTED
10 DEC 72 .... KORAT RTAFB / ARRIVED
27 DEC 72 .... KORAT RTAFB / DEPARTED
27 DEC 72 .... UBON RTAFB / ARRIVED
27 DEC 72 .... UBON RTAFB / DEPARTED
27 DEC 72 .... NAKHON PHANOM RTAFB / ARRIVED
27 DEC 72 .... NAKHON PHANOM (NKP) RTAFB / DEPARTED
27 DEC 72 .... UDORN RTAFB / ARRIVED
29 DEC 72 .... UDORN RTAFB / DEPARTED
29 DEC 72 .... NKP RTAFB / ARRIVED
29 DEC 72 .... NKP RTAFB / DEPARTED
29 DEC 72 .... UBON RTAFB / ARRIVED
29 DEC 72 .... UBON RTAFB / DEPARTED
29 DEC 72 .... KORAT RTAFB / ARRIVED
16 JAN 73 .... KORAT RTAFB / DEPARTED
16 JAN 73 .... KADENA OKINAWA / ARRIVED

16 JAN 73....................KADENA OKINAWA / DEPARTED
16 JAN 73....................HICKAM AFB HAW / ARRIVED
16 JAN 73....................HICKAM AFB HAW / DEPARTED
16 JAN 73....................NORTON AFB CAL / ARRIVED
16 JAN 73....................NORTON AFB CAL / DEPARTED
16 JAN 73....................ENGLAND AFB LA. / ARRIVED

OTHER ADDRESSES:

2107 MOHO DRIVE, ORLANDO FLA. 2 SEPT 1963
BASE VIEW TRAILER COURT, EMERADO NDAK. LOT N-22, 28
    SEP 1963
1507 NIMROD LANE, ORLANDO FLA. 14 AUG 1967
VAGABOND MOBILE LODGE RT. 5, LUBBOCK TX. 05 SEP 1967
REESE AFB LOT A-6, LUBBOCK TX. 06 JUNE 1969
RT. 15, BOX 580-A LOT 3, ORLANDO FLA. 16 JULY 1970
RT. 5, BOX 580-A LOT 3, ORLANDO FLA. 16 JULY 1970
3465 BENSON HIGHWAY, US. 80, TUCSON ARIZ. 25 JULY 1970
LOT 6, ENGLAND AFB. LA. AUGUST 1972

Chapter 9
Retirement

After returning from Korat to England Air Force Base, Alexandria, Louisiana, I cross-trained into Ground Safety for the remaining four years. That is comparable to Occupational Safety and Health but using air force regulations. In 1979 I started working at Pinecrest State School as their safety coordinator to establish a safety program. At night I attended college courses at Northwestern State University offsite on England Air Force Base to complete my BA using the GI Bill. In 1985 I started working with the Louisiana Department of Health and Hospitals as a surveyor. *Surveyor* is a fancy term for inspector. HCFA training included fire safety and general regulations for inspecting Medicare and Medicaid funded facilities, such as hospitals and nursing homes. That's a story in and of itself. I retired from the Louisiana Department of Health and Hospitals in 2001.

About the Author

Born on Fort Bragg Army Base, North Carolina. His father was a sergeant in the US Army, and after twenty-eight years he retired as a major. In 1948, he accompanied his parents to Germany as part of occupation forces, where he learned to speak German sufficiently to translate for his parents. During the three years in Germany, he visited many surrounding countries. He returned to the United States in 1953 with his family. In 1958, he graduated from Columbia Military Academy, Columbia, Tennessee, and enlisted in the US Air Force that same year. After three tours to Vietnam, he cross-trained into Ground Safety for his four remaining years until he retired from the air force in 1978. He then used his GI Bill to finish college and graduated from Northwest State University, Natchitoches, Louisiana, in 1983. He started civilian life working as the safety coordinator for Pinecrest State School in Pineville, Louisiana. After six years, he transferred and started working as a surveyor (inspector) for the Louisiana Department of Health and Hospitals, inspecting Medicare and Medicaid facilities, hospitals, and nursing homes. In 1992, he completed a master's degree in management at England Air Force Base extension, from Webster's University in Saint Louis, Missouri. He retired again in 2001 from the state of Louisiana and then worked part time for the Louisiana Board of Wholesale Drug Distributors. In 2003, he was elected as one of the directors for Rapides Island Water Association by the members. In 2013, he retired from both of them. Currently, he is a volunteer for CASA (Court Appointed Special Advocates) for children. Occasionally writes gibes for cenlapatriots.org (search Jim Downey).